INDUS

RELATIONS

& POLITICS

IN BRITAIN

1880-1989

JOHN SHELDRAKE

Pinter Publishers
London and New York

© John Sheldrake 1991

First published in Great Britain in 1991 by
Pinter Publishers Limited
25 Floral Street, London WC2E 9DS

British Library Cataloguing in Publication Data

A CIP catalogue record for this book is available from the
British Library
ISBN 0–86187 – 814 – 0 Hbk
      0–86187 – 815 – 9 Ppr

Library of Congress Cataloging in Publication Data
A CIP catalog record for this book is
available from the Library of Congress

Typeset by Selectmove Ltd
Printed and bound in Great Britain by Billing and Sons,
Worcester

'We have no guide to the future
except our experience of the past.'

Lord Askwith

Contents

Acronyms and Abbreviations

AEU	Amalgamated Engineering Union
ASE	Amalgamated Society of Engineers
BOAC	British Overseas Airways Corporation
EETPU	Electrical, Electronic, Telecommunications and Plumbing Union
EPEA	Electrical Power Engineers Association
GMB	General, Municipal and Boilermakers' Union
ILP	Independent Labour Party
ISTC	Iron and Steel Trades Confederation
LCC	London County Council
MATSA	Managerial, Administrative, Technical and Supervisory Association
LRC	Labour Representation Committee
MLNS	Ministry of Labour and National Service
NALGO	National and Local Government Officers Association
NCB	National Coal Board
NJIC	National Joint Industrial Council
NRA	National Rivers Authority
NUGGL	National Union of Gasworkers and General Labourers
NUM	National Union of Miners
NUPE	National Union of Public Employees
NWC	National Water Council
PLC	Public Limited Company
RWA	Regional Water Authority
SDF	Social Democratic Federation
SIC	Special Industrial Committee of the TUC
TGWU	Transport and General Workers Union
TUC	Trades Union Congress
UCATT	Union of Construction, Allied Trades and Technicians
UDM	Union of Democratic Miners
WAA	Water Authorities Association
WCA	Water Companies Association

Chapter 1

Introduction

This book aims to provide a concise account of the impact of industrial relations on British politics during the last hundred years or so. It is centrally concerned with possibilities, policies, policy outcomes, electoral consequences and the perceptions of politicians and electors. It is also interested in the extent to which policies implemented in one set of circumstances subsequently limit the scope for alternative policies and ultimately ramify into habit, custom and tradition. A central theme therefore is the gradual accretion of government responsibility for industrial relations which culminated in the crisis of 1979 and generated the opportunity for the radically different approach adopted by the governments of Margaret Thatcher. A book of this kind cannot of course be exhaustive and, although it is designed to be non-partisan, the author's prejudices and idiosyncrasies will inevitably show through. Equally such a book must be a product of its times, particularly when it comes to analysing the significance of recent events. Had it, for example, been written in 1980 it would no doubt have concluded that legislation calculated to reduce the scope of trade union activity would be unlikely to succeed. It would also have argued that any political party presiding over historically high levels of unemployment would definitely be punished at the ballot box. By contrast, had it been completed in 1989, it might have concluded that decisive changes had been wrought in British industrial relations, leading to radical improvements in the performance of the economy and halting the country's relative decline. Writing in 1990, however, any such certainty is inappropriate. That there have been significant changes over the past ten years goes without saying. To conclude that they are decisive, or that Britain has finally overcome its industrial relations and economic difficulties would be far more problematical. This book therefore ends on a note of hesitancy concerning likely future developments which, given the author's own views, is highly appropriate.

The material contained in the chapters which follow is presented thematically and more or less chronologically. The major sources of the material can be found in the notes at the end of each chapter and also the bibliography. Chapter 2 covers relevant legislative developments from the mid-1870s up to the period immediately preceding the First World War, including the extension of trade union immunities, attempts to stimulate voluntary conciliation and the limited imposition of trade board protection. Developments in the trade union movement, the influence of various ideologies, the impact of industrial unrest and the emergence of the Labour Party as a political force are also examined. The chapter details the creation of the Labour Department of the Board of Trade and its work in encouraging the development of collective bargaining. Finally, consideration is given to the work of the Industrial Council. Chapter 3 deals with the rapid changes in politics and industrial relations stimulated by the First World War. The role of the Committee on Production is examined together with that of the Ministries of Munitions, Labour and Reconstruction. The rapid growth of the trade union movement is noted and the tensions generated by dilution and the emergence of the shop stewards' movement are considered. The chapter also details the work of the Whitley Committee and notes the influence of its reports on the widespread establishment of National Joint Industrial Councils, the extension of trade board protection and the creation of the Industrial Court. Finally, the immediate aftermath of the war is examined with specific reference to the influence of the Cave Committee.

Chapter 4 covers the period from the end of the First World War to the election of the first majority Labour Government in 1945. The consequences of economic recession are examined, particularly the effects of high unemployment including the numerical decline of the trade unions. Further, the origins and outcomes of the 1926 General Strike are considered. The influence of the Ministry of Labour, especially in the sphere of industrial training, is detailed and its expanded role as the Ministry of Labour and National Service noted. Finally, an account is given of the corporatist structure of industrial relations which developed during the Second World War. Chapter 5 examines the development of what is often described as the post-war political consensus and its demise under the impact of economic decline and industrial conflict. Attempts by government to intervene in industrial relations through incomes policy and legislation restricting the scope of trade union activity are considered, together with the brief vogue for productivity bargaining. Government's efforts to grapple with the problems posed by rapidly rising inflation and unemployment are also detailed. The chapter concludes with the defeat of Labour in May 1979 and the return of the Conservatives under the leadership of Margaret Thatcher. Chapter 6 provides an account of the alternative approach to industrial relations issues which has operated under the Thatcher Governments since 1979. The influence of high levels of unemployment, the abandonment of incomes policy and attempts to achieve labour market flexibility are considered, together with the piecemeal introduction of legislation which has systematically reduced trade union immunities. Privatisation, contracting-out provisions and the government inspired attack on national collective bargaining are also examined. An account of the miners' strike 1984–5 is given. Finally, a case study of recent developments in industrial relations in the water industry provides an opportunity to consider a situation where privatisation and an end to national collective bargaining have developed in tandem. Chapter 7 provides a summing up and a consideration of likely future developments.

I would like to acknowledge the assistance I have received in the preparation of this book from the Public Records Office at Kew, the Imperial War Museum Library, the TUC Library, the Department of Employment Library, the Water Services Association Library, and the City of London Polytechnic Library at Calcutta House. I would also like to acknowledge the many discussions on matters of industrial relations and politics which I have had with colleagues and students during the ten years that I have been working on the subject matter contained in this book. In particular I would mention John Donaldson, Sarah Vickerstaff, Michael Woodcock, Rene Saran, Geoffrey Stuttard, Rodney Dobson, Geoffrey Roberts, Howard Gospel, John Lovell, Richard Cook, John McGuire and Christopher Trinder. Finally, I would like to thank my wife, Susan for her advice on numerous points of detail and her tireless efforts in preparing the typescript.

Leigh-on-Sea
July 1990

Chapter 2

Industrial Unrest and the Rise of Labour

By 1880 the trade unions had obtained legislative protection for their funds and the bulk of their activities. The Conspiracy and Protection of Property Act 1875 permitted peaceful picketing and also provided that acts committed in furtherance of a trade dispute should no longer be considered a criminal conspiracy unless the actions were in themselves criminal. That the unions had gained protection under the law was largely due to the success of their leaders at the Royal Commission on Trade Unions established in 1867. The Royal Commission was prompted by the 'Sheffield outrages'; acts of violence and intimidation perpetrated by the Sheffield trade societies as a means of disciplining members. The London-based leaders of the amalgamated (New Model) unions, the so-called 'Junta'[1], represented their organizations as bastions of artisan respectability. In particular Robert Applegarth, of the Amalgamated Society of Carpenters and Joiners, succeeded in convincing the Commission that, far from being a threat, properly managed trade unions were a means of obtaining harmonious industrial relations. The activities of the Sheffield societies were depicted as an outmoded anachronism left over from the era of Luddism and bearing little relation to the moderation displayed by the New Model unions. Applegarth and his colleagues were assisted in their efforts by sympathetic members of the Commission such as the Christian Socialist, Thomas Hughes and their own nominee the Positivist, Frederic Harrison. Further, A. J. Mundella, a self-made Nottingham hosiery manufacturer, who was soon to become Liberal MP for Sheffield and having pioneered arbitration and conciliation boards, was highly supportive of responsible trade unionism. Mundella saw collective bargaining as the means to obviate industrial unrest and, speaking as a large employer of labour, he informed the Commission that the leaders of the New Model unions had 'been the greatest barriers we have had between the ignorant workmen and ourselves'.[2]

The patent decency of Applegarth and his colleagues was persuasive in prompting the political nation to accept and legitimise trade union activity. Equally, the extension of the franchise to the artisanate determined that, henceforth, politicians must legislate in a manner calculated to attract the, albeit limited, working class vote. One outcome of the extended franchise was the establishment of the Parliamentary Committee of the TUC in 1871. Under the Secretaryship of George Howell it undertook the task of lobbying for legislative reforms beneficial to organized labour which resulted in the successful passage of the 1875 Act. A further outcome was the entry of the first working men into Parliament in 1874. Thomas Burt, a Northumberland miner, was elected for Morpeth alongside Alexander Macdonald, the leader of the miners' union, for Stafford – both were Liberals who became the first of the so called Lib-Labs.

The craft unions organized on the basis of the New Model (with high subscriptions, restricted entry, extensive friendly society benefits and national organization) were concerned as much with protecting their trades against unskilled interlopers as they were with defending their position against the encroachment of employers. Central to their strategy was the limitation of entry into the craft by the use of apprenticeship and, whatever their reputation for moderation and respectability, they were fierce in their determination to defend their craft against dilution. By limiting the numbers entering the craft, unions such as the Amalgamated Society of Engineers (ASE) were able to influence the supply of entrants and maintain a modicum of control over the labour process. As foreign competition increased, however, and new machinery and management techniques were introduced, the engineers were forced into protracted struggles to defend their position on the workshop floor. Although unions of a less exclusive nature than the skill-based organizations developed in, for example, the cotton and coalmining industries, the pre-eminence of the New Model unions created a situation where organized labour in Britain became characterised at an early stage by the domination of sectional interest over class solidarity.

New unionism and socialism

The leaders of the New Model unions did not seek to disrupt or greatly disturb the social and political status quo. The development of industry and urbanisation created areas where social stratification manifested itself in communities that were wholly working class and where contact with members of other classes was limited or non-existent. Within the vast working-class enclaves the significant social distinctions were between groups within the working class rather than between that class and others. Although major legislative reforms beneficial to the working class, including the Conspiracy and Protection of Property Act, were carried out by the Conservatives the enfranchised artisanate gave its support to the Liberals. As will be seen, however, political realignments were developing which were to re-shape working-class and, indeed, British politics generally during the thirty or so years after 1880.

During the last quarter of the nineteenth century collectivist notions increasingly challenged the ideological hegemony hitherto enjoyed by individualism. The problems generated by industrialisation and urbanisation (not least the constant threat of epidemic disease) stimulated piecemeal state intervention across a range of activities. Many of these interventions increased the influence of the local authorities whose gradual appropriation of the public utilities gave rise to the notion of 'gas and water' or municipal socialism. Inspired by the activities of Joseph Chamberlain in Birmingham and the developments in municipal ownership in, for example, Liverpool and Manchester, Sidney Webb and other members of the Fabian Society put forward a vision of gradual collectivism. In *Fabian Essays*, published in

1889 to coincide with the establishment of the London County Council (LCC), Webb reviewed the historical basis of socialism and emphasised its unconscious development under the impact of continuous municipalisation. State intervention, collectivism and socialism were depicted as part of an irreversible process destined to provide a more efficient and equal society. The Fabians' views were paralleled by the Idealist philosophy of T. H. Green which characterised the state as both a central and positive element in social life. The work of Green underpinned the New Liberalism which abandoned the nostrums of *laissez faire* and looked to piecemeal state intervention as the means to ameliorate social injustice. As Sabine and Thorson have observed, the ideas of the Fabians and Green

reflected, probably independently, an important change in the climate of British political opinion, namely, a loss of confidence in the alleged efficiency of private enterprise and an increased willingness to use the state's legislative and administrative power to correct its abuses and harmonise it.[3]

The Fabian Society provided one element in the three-fold development of socialist organizations which occurred during the 1880s and early 1890s. Together with the Marxist inspired Social Democratic Federation (SDF) and the Independent Labour Party (ILP), the Fabians urged a fundamental shift in the basis of social and economic organization. Favourable economic circumstances together with associated industrial unrest created the opportunity for the ideological assertions of the socialist societies to inspire a new generation of militant trade unionists. Whereas the cautious leaders of the New Model unions had been broadly content to accept the social status quo, the new generation, armed with socialist thought, were prepared to advocate a complete social transformation either through peaceful or revolutionary means. Just as the reformists of the New Model unions had felt a kinship with Gladstonian Liberalism, so the new generation felt an identification with socialism and the achievement of an independent labour presence in Parliament. This is not, of course, to suggest that the generality of match-girls, gas stokers and dockers who took part in the industrial unrest of 1888 and

1889 were inspired by much other than bread and butter issues such as better working conditions, reduced working hours or increased pay. Nevertheless the feeling grew among elements of both the middle and working classes that the many need not of necessity remain poor and also that the existing political parties were not equal to bringing about fundamental change.

The serious industrial unrest of 1888 and 1889 was geographically concentrated in the Docklands area of East London where labour conditions were mainly characterised by small scale sweated industry and the casualisation associated with dock work. Unionisation had made little impact among the unskilled labour force of the East End where pressures of immigration, poor housing and poverty largely precluded the possibility of organization on New Model lines. The strikes at Bryant and May's match factory, the Gas Light and Coke Company's Beckton works and in the docks were characterised by a new partnership of militant working-class leaders and radical middle-class sympathisers. Both groups were inspired by the revival of socialist ideas and were often affiliated to one or other of the socialist societies. The appalling working conditions of the match-girls, for example, were exposed by the Fabian Annie Besant while Will Thorne, himself a Beckton gas stoker, was assisted by Eleanor Marx. Thorne, together with prominent organizers of the dock strike such as Tom Mann and John Burns, was a member of the SDF.

Militant industrial action was paralleled in London by a ferment of radical ideas and the success of the strikes due not only to industrial muscle but also to a climate of public opinion sympathetic to the strikers' claims. The establishment of the LCC, and the awareness that the capital lagged behind the great provincial cities in terms of governance and the provision of public amenities, had concentrated the attention of radicals and reformers on the social problems of the East End. The publication of the first volume of Charles Booth's *London Life and Labour* generated a programme of welfare legislation, designed to mitigate the worst aspects of poverty, which became common ground among socialists and New Liberals. The ability of the unskilled workers of the East End to organize themselves for strike activity both surprised and impressed middle-class sympathisers. As Beatrice Webb confided in her diary 'East End society has suddenly ... roused itself to struggle against an evil growing in its midst to which it has shown itself hitherto absolutely apathetic and indifferent, and has proved itself more capable of concerted action than any other district in England'.[4] The discipline and moderation of the dockers was impressive as they marched daily from Docklands to Tower Hill where they were addressed by Mann, Burns and Ben Tillett, and returned via the City. As Pelling has observed 'the sight of this enormous but completely orderly host of determined men, walking five abreast, impressed public opinion and won many generous contributions to the strike funds'.[5]

Success in the London strikes stimulated the spread of unionisation of unskilled workers beyond the capital and into industries outside gas and the docks. Two of the unions that emerged at this time – the Dock, Wharf, Riverside and General Workers Union and the National Union of Gasworkers and General Labourers (NUGGL) – formed the basis of today's great general unions – the TGWU and the GMB. Whereas the craft unions associated with the New Model had based their strength on craft exclusiveness, high subscriptions and extensive friendly society benefits the so-called 'new unionism' of the unskilled was based on a desire to unionise all workers rather than a particular stratum. Subscriptions were therefore low, entry to the union easy and, in the early days at least, industrial militancy more commonplace. Membership of the new unions was, however, perishable and although growth was rapid during the economic boom of 1889–90 it was not sustained in the depressed conditions of the 1890s. Lovell has observed that by the end of the 1890s the new unions accounted for less than one tenth of total trade union membership.[6] The new unions had, of course, to contend with a vigorous counter attack by employers. In the gas industry, for example, Sir George Livesey, chairman of London's South Metropolitan Gas Company succeeded in removing the NUGGL from his works in 1890 and, as late as 1906, was able to boast that no trade union had any influence in his company. Livesey became an advocate of 'free (i.e. non-union) labour' and matched resistance to trade union recognition with an enlightened programme of co-partnership and profit-sharing.

In contrast to Livesey, David Milne Watson, the chairman of London's massive Gas Light and Coke Company, continued to negotiate with the NUGGL and was instrumental in sustaining orderly industrial relations in the gas industry. Indeed Will Thorne and Milne Watson continued joint negotiations up until Thorne's retirement in 1934 – a period of 45 years.

Socialism does not possess a unitary meaning and it is easy to lapse into anachronism when attempting to assess the nature of the socialist programme put forward by the socialist societies during the 1890s. Equally it is easy to overrate the novelty of the new unionism. In practical terms the socialism of the 1890s may be broadly equated to an expansion of the role of the state, a growing enthusiasm for collectivism and a determination to get more working men into Parliament. Further, although the initial impact of the new unions was felt as a radicalising influence within the TUC, their goals ultimately mirrored those of the old unions. Many of the ambitions of the socialists coincided with those of the New Liberals and differed only in terms of ideological rhetoric. The Fabians, for example, supported the Progressives (an alliance of Liberals, radicals, religious philanthropists and trade unions) on the LCC and Sidney Webb himself was elected as Progressive candidate for Deptford in 1892. Most importantly perhaps the rise of the new unionism had the effect of linking the advancement of socialist objectives with the fortunes of the trade unions. A growing awareness of the inability of the Liberal Party to deliver legislation beneficial to the working class, coupled with the reluctance of local parties to select working men as parliamentary candidates, stimulated interest in the creation of a new political party able to represent the political and industrial arms of the labour movement. However, when such a party finally emerged it took much of the political ground, including an absolute acceptance of parliamentary democracy, as it found it. In terms of more radical or revolutionary aspirations the linkage of socialism to the trade union movement ensured that such aspirations were more or less doomed from the start.

In 1899 the TUC approved a resolution from the Amalgamated Society of Railway Servants calling for a conference of socialist, co-operative and trade union organizations to discuss ways of getting more labour representatives into Parliament. As Hinton has observed 'this had the advantage of leaving those (unions) who preferred to rely on their own political resources, notably the big batallions of coal and cotton, free to do so, while allowing those unions who favoured a pooling of resources to proceed independently of the remainder'.[7] The Parliamentary Committee of the TUC duly called a conference on 27 February 1900 at the Memorial Hall in Farringdon Street, London. The Fabian Society, the SDF and the ILP were in attendance together with trade union representatives from about half of those affiliated to the TUC. At the conference the SDF agitated for a commitment to Marxist objectives while the Lib-Labs attempted to limit discussions to the reformist policies of the trade unions. In the event, prompted by Keir Hardie and the ILP, a compromise was reached and it was agreed that a distinct group should be established in Parliament charged with the promotion of legislation favourable to the interests of labour. The outcome of the conference was the establishment of the Labour Representation Committee (LRC) – forerunner of the modern Labour Party.

A government department for labour

A. J. Mundella became President of the Board of Trade in February 1886 and established a labour bureau charged with the collection and dissemination of labour statistics. As we have seen, as well as being a businessman and a politician, Mundella was a veteran campaigner for industrial arbitration and conciliation and also sympathetic to responsible trade unionism. He had been impressed by the success of the labour boards in the United States which had been used to inform workers there about both the economic situation in that country and the strength of foreign competition. Eager to strengthen links between the Liberal Party and the TUC, he chose John Burnett, General Secretary of the ASE and a trade union moderate, to become the first labour correspondent. Burnett set up a network of correspondents in the country's major industrial centres and began to collect intelligence on strikes and lockouts which was published in detailed annual reports. Although Mundella went out of office with the fall of Gladstone's government in July 1886, he resumed his duties in August 1892 and, in 1893, established the Labour Department of the Board of Trade – forerunner of the Ministry of Labour and the Department of Employment.

The first Commissioner of the Department was a young radical, not yet thirty years of age, called Hubert Llewellyn Smith. He pioneered a pragmatic, empirical approach to industrial relations problems, rose to become Permanent Secretary of the Board of Trade in 1907 and was responsible, with Lloyd George and Christopher Addison, for the successful creation and operation of the Ministry of Munitions during the First World War. The son of a Quaker tea merchant in Bristol he was imbued with a spirit of social idealism having gone to Oxford in 1883 and fallen under the influence of T. H. Green. At Oxford Llewellyn Smith had joined a group known as the 'Inner Ring' that concerned itself with the social, political and economic questions of the day and was convened by the radical Arthur Acland. During 1886 this group was addressed by John Burnett and the experience kindled Llewellyn Smith's interest in the problems of industrial relations. In 1888 he joined Toynbee Hall, the university's settlement in East London, and assisted Annie Besant in leading the Bryant and May's match-girls to victory in their strike. He also helped Charles Booth with his survey and worked behind the scenes in the London dock strike about which, together with Vaughan Nash, he subsequently wrote a history. Between 1888 and 1893 Llewellyn Smith built up a formidable network of contacts in radical and labour circles including Ben Tillett, John Burns and Tom Mann. He also collaborated with the Webbs in promoting social reforms especially in the sphere of technical education. Although his contacts were with organized labour and Liberal progressives, once appointed as Commissioner he was careful to establish a reputation for neutrality, distancing himself from the work of the Webbs which he characterised as political propaganda.

Llewellyn Smith's work at the Labour Department was crucial in advancing progressive ideas on industrial relations issues in the period up to 1916. Under the auspices of the Permanent Secretary of the Board of Trade, Sir Courtenay Boyle, he assembled an impressive group of specialist statisticians and labour economists whose work was published monthly in the *Labour Gazette*. It was on the basis of its work in the area of labour statistics that the Labour Department initially built its reputation. Further, its ability to provide accurate statistical information influenced government in deciding to place the Conciliation Act 1896 under the aegis of the Board of Trade rather than the Home Office. Similarly, the Department's statistical investigations into the problems of sweated labour were crucial when responsibility for the trade boards was given to the Board of Trade in 1909. It was the Labour Department which pioneered and maintained a confidence in voluntary collective bargaining by employers associations and trade unions organized as joint boards. Allied to this was the advocacy of state-supported, voluntary conciliation and a deep suspicion of compulsory arbitration. The thrust of these opinions was that the establishment of voluntary collective bargaining machinery would serve to minimise serious industrial conflict by creating the habit of negotiation.

The question of trade union immunities

Initial trade union enthusiasm for the LRC was moderate but increased as a result of the House of Lords' decision in the Taff Vale case in July 1901. This judgement determined that trade unions could be sued for damages inflicted by their officials and undermined the apparent immunities obtained under the legal settlement of 1875. As Phelps Brown has observed 'the right to strike, intact in principle, was nullified in practice'.[8] The response of the unions to the situation was, as far as possible, to refrain from taking strike action and seek an early change in the law. Following the Taff Vale decision affiliation to the LRC was rapid, increasing from under 400,000 in June 1901 to almost 850,000 in February 1903. By 1905 only the coalminers, remaining loyal to their Lib-Lab commitments, stood aside from the growing trade union determination to increase the strength of the LRC.

Trade union support for the LRC sprang essentially from the desire to obtain changes in the law rather than any commitment to socialist objectives. In general terms, the bulk of the unions did not desire an alternative to Liberalism but merely the creation of a force capable of persuading the next Liberal government to reverse the effects of Taff Vale. The rapid growth of the LRC's membership impressed the Liberal Party and stimulated a desire to avoid three-cornered fights in marginal constituencies. The outcome was an electoral pact concluded between the Liberal Party's Chief Whip, Herbert Gladstone, and Ramsay MacDonald, the Secretary of the LRC, that allowed a free run to thirty LRC candidates. In 1905 Joseph Chamberlain split the Conservative Party on the issue of tariff reform and the Prime Minister, Arthur Balfour, resigned without dissolving Parliament. This move signalled a revival of Liberal Party fortunes and its leader, Campbell-Bannerman, formed an interim government. In the election of January 1906 the Liberals won a landslide victory at the polls and the LRC returned twenty-nine members many of whom were trade union leaders. The LRC renamed itself the Labour Party, elected Keir Hardie as its parliamentary leader, appointed its own whips and began to agitate for legislation favourable to organized labour.

The previous government had appointed a Royal Commission under the chairmanship of Lord Dunedin, in June 1903, to examine the question of trade union immunities. The Commission reported in January 1906 and the newly elected government introduced a Trade Disputes Bill, calculated to reverse the effects of Taff Vale, and based broadly on the Commission's recommendations. The government's bill did not propose to make trade unions directly immune from actions at tort. Instead, it proposed that unions should appoint executive committees for the conduct of disputes and take legal responsibility only for actions authorised by these committees. This bill did not, however, satisfy the trade unions who introduced a private member's Labour Bill calculated to provide them with complete immunity from actions at tort. Although the law officers and the lawyers in the Cabinet were frankly aghast at giving such immunity to the unions, and even a trade union sympathiser such as Sidney Webb was averse to the idea, the simplicity of the Labour Bill was attractive to the Prime Minister and also to Parliament in general. The text of the Labour Bill was thus substituted for that of the government's bill and went to the

House of Lords in that form. The upper chamber, apparently shrinking from further alienating the trade unions, did not seek to revise the proposed legislation which passed into law as the Trades Disputes Act 1906 and provided the unions with complete immunity for actions at tort. Just as the 1875 Act had placed strike action beyond the scope of criminal conspiracy so the 1906 Act placed such action beyond the scope of civil conspiracy.

The campaign for trade board protection

The campaign for trade boards or wages councils, charged with the fixing of minimum pay levels, had its origins in a growing public concern about the problems of sweated industry during the 1880s. In 1885 a severe trade depression directed public attention to the low wages and bad working conditions of the lowest paid groups of workers. The issue was investigated by a select committee of the House of Lords under the chairmanship of Lord Dunraven which reported in 1890 and defined 'sweating' as 'inadequate wages, inordinately long hours, and insanitary conditions of labour'.[9] The committee's major recommendations proposed amendments to the Factory and Public Health Acts as a means of improving conditions of work. A suggestion, by the chainmakers, that legally enforceable minimum rates be established was dismissed by the Lords as unthinkable as it ran counter to accepted notions of the inviolability of the market. In the event the select committee's recommendations were not implemented although there developed a growing awareness of the need, as Beatrice Webb expressed it, to 'secure to every worker prescribed minimum conditions of employment'.[10] This view was made manifest in the First Fair Wages Resolution of the House of Commons in 1891 which established the principle that the terms and conditions of employment of employees of government contractors should not be inferior to those of the government employees in the trade or industry in the district concerned. In 1900 Sir Charles Dilke introduced a Sweated Industries Bill which, although it made no progress in the House of Commons, signalled the opening of the long campaign to achieve legal protection for the most vulnerable and exploited members of the work force.

The problem of sweated labour was not, of course, confined to Britain. Wages boards charged with setting minimum rates of pay were introduced in Australia in 1895 and, in Germany, the products of sweated labour were exhibited as a means of gaining publicity for the cause of reform. Both of these initiatives inspired and influenced the campaign for reform in Britain. In the summer of 1906, the *Daily News* (edited by the radical A. G. Gardiner) sponsored an exhibition of sweated goods produced by shirt-makers, fur sewers, tennis and racket ball makers, lace-workers, chainmakers and garment workers generally. The majority of these workers were women and the campaign against sweated labour became increasingly linked with the general campaign for female emancipation. Following the *Daily News* exhibition a pressure group was formed, the National Anti-Sweating League, which took as its objective the establishment of a statutory minimum wage. A conference on the subject was held at the Guildhall and addressed by Mary Macarthur, secretary of the National Federation of Women Workers, which took a leading part in the campaign for protective legislation. The main thrust of her argument was an attempt to convince employers that 'sweating' favoured the bad, low cost employer and that minimum wage legislation would assist good employers by obviating the need to compete on the basis of wage rates alone. As the campaign developed prominent Labour leaders, such as Arthur Henderson and David Shackleton, became enthusiastic advocates of trade boards and the success of the Labour Party in the 1906 election stimulated pressure for a parliamentary select committee to enquire into the subject of sweated industry.

In 1908 the select committee of the House of Commons on Home Work recommended the adoption of the general principle of legal minimum time and piece rates for homeworkers and advocated legislation on an experimental basis. Meanwhile, a special commissioner was despatched to Australia to observe and then report to the British government on the working of wages boards in that country. When legislation was produced it was a compromise measure introduced by Winston Churchill in his capacity as President of the Board of Trade, and the provisions of what became the Trade Boards Act 1909 were severely limited.

Only four trades were covered, viz. chainmaking, machine-made lace and net finishing, paper box making and wholesale tailoring. The initial trades were selected to be widely differing in order to test the effect of legal interventions but power was given to the President of the Board of Trade to schedule other trades by Provisional Order to be confirmed by Parliament. In 1913 four more trades were scheduled, viz. sugar confectionery and food preserving, shirt-making, hollow-ware and tin box making, and linen and cotton embroidery. These eight boards covered about half a million workers. Although the 1909 Act was limited in its scope and impact it nevertheless formed a significant departure from the conventions of voluntarism which had hitherto dominated British industrial relations and marked a significant intervention on the part of government.

Labour unrest and the influence of syndicalism

In the years between 1910 and the outbreak of the First World War there occurred a period of bitter industrial unrest the main cause of which lay in a continued drop in real wages. Labour unrest was paralleled by lack of harmony and cohesion in the trade union movement as unions developed in a haphazard manner and proliferated without plan. As MacDonald has observed 'there might be a score of them elbowing and snarling at each other in the same industry'.[11] Further, although trade union membership grew steadily from under 1 million in 1888 to over 2 million in 1906 and increased to over 4 million by 1913, industrial unrest often broke out before union organization in the industries concerned could cope with it. Although the major motive for the unrest was certainly economic it was fuelled and articulated by the imported ideas of syndicalism and industrial unionism.

Syndicalism originated in the industrial areas of France and Belgium during the 1890s and drew its theoretical content from the writings of Proudhon and Marx. In practical terms it meant workers' control of industry. The existing centralised political system was to be replaced by a federalised structure based on local organizations of producers. This replacement would occur either gradually or as a result of a revolutionary crisis culminating in a general strike. Following the overthrow of the existing order industry in each locality would be run by the unions and, over larger areas, by a general labour federation. Industrial unionism, the American counterpart of European syndicalism, was advocated by the Industrial Workers of the World and encouraged by Daniel de Leon's Socialist Labour Party. A British branch of this movement was founded in 1903 by the Irish labour leader James Conolly and, from 1910 onwards, Tom Mann introduced French and American notions of workers' control into Britain through his journal *Industrial Syndicalist*. After 1912 a diluted form of syndicalism was advocated by the Guild Socialists who claimed that the government of industry should involve all those concerned with production, including managerial and professional elements, rather than only manual workers. A further refinement was provided by G. D. H. Cole in his *The World of Labour* which drew on insights from Ruskin and Morris.

In its extreme form syndicalism viewed trade unions as the means for achieving socialism and depicted the general strike as the weapon which would abolish capitalist society. In its reformist version it adopted a strategy of encroaching control whereby gradual advances on the workshop floor would wrest prerogatives from management. Critics have doubted the achievements of syndicalist ideology but there is no doubt of its lasting influence in trade union circles. The notion of the general strike remained a potent threat for many years after syndicalism was forgotten and the notion of encroaching control continued as a feature of shop floor trade union activity. In the context of the industrial unrest preceding the First World War, syndicalist propaganda stressed the benefits of industrial unionism over sectionalism and challenged the moderation of the established trade union leadership with the claims of a militant rank and file. Growth in the influence of syndicalism among the working class was assisted by the severe financial difficulties experienced by the Labour Party in the period following the Osborne Judgement in 1909 which were not remedied until the passage of the Trade Union Act in 1913. While the Labour Party remained in the doldrums direct action appeared to offer a greater potential for social and political change than did parliamentary representation.

The main focus of the strikes was in coalmining, railways and the docks although other industries, such as boilermaking, cotton and jute, were also involved. Industrial unrest was often accompanied by severe civil disturbance with injuries, loss of life, attacks on property and the widespread deployment of police reinforcements and the military. In June 1911, for example, a strike of dockers in Hull brought arson, looting and rioting to the city on a scale which an eyewitness described as worse than he had seen in Paris during the days of the Commune. Similarly, in Manchester, when a transport strike paralysed the city, police were drafted in from Birmingham and, following disturbances, troops occupied the neighbouring town of Salford. In Liverpool a strike of railwaymen, supported by unofficial action from other transport workers, brought the city to a standstill and two people were killed when troops opened fire on a rioting mob. The Liberal Government of Herbert Asquith responded as best it could to the troubles – sometimes seeking to placate the strikers, sometimes uttering dire warnings and finally, as war with Germany became an increasing possibility, appealing to the strikers' sense of patriotism. Most often, however, the government fell back on the efforts of their conciliator George Askwith to obtain negotiated settlements. Askwith was a barrister with a reputation for patience, stamina, neutrality and a refusal to panic in the face of hostility and severe civil disturbance. His painstaking method of negotiation was demonstrated in the Manchester transport strike where he conducted five days of constant, parallel meetings before hammering out a settlement. As he noted in his memoirs:

In every room in the Town Hall, which the Lord Mayor had put at our disposal, different trades were closeted, employers and employed, debating, discussing, and almost fighting. Hour by hour and day by day, it was possible to go from one to the other, get a dispute upon apparent lines of possible settlement, and then answer a hurried summons to another room to prevent a conference breaking up.[12]

The ferocity of the industrial unrest, particularly as it affected Manchester, and Askwith's success in resolving the dispute, stimulated Sir Charles Macara to call for the establishment of a 'business court'. Macara was the longstanding chairman of the employers federation in the cotton industry and had experienced the value of industrial conciliation. He took the view that a 'business court' should be constituted of prominent employers and trade union leaders, meeting under an independent chairman experienced in industrial relations matters such as George Askwith. Disputes would be referred to the court before a strike or lockout occurred and Macara believed that, although the court's findings would not be legally binding on the parties, they would prove to be sufficiently persuasive to substantially reduce the level of unrest. There was little originality in Macara's proposal. The influence of Mundella has been noted and the desirability of fostering conciliation had been affirmed by the Devonshire Commission (1891–1894) and made manifest in the Conciliation Act 1896. This Act provided that the Board of Trade might inquire into the causes and circumstances of industrial disputes and make provision for conciliation and arbitration. Although the operation of the Act had proved difficult during the period of employer counter attack against the trade unions during the late 1890s and early 1900s, the idea of conciliation had gained growing acceptance and, by 1911, there were over 300 conciliation boards in existence. These boards were seen as an answer to local problems. The novelty of Macara's proposal was in its assertion of the need to establish a national, standing body capable of addressing itself to major industrial disputes likely to disrupt trade beyond the immediate confines of the industry concerned.

In the circumstances of 1911 Macara's proposal appeared to offer at least the possibility of dealing with industrial disputes in a coherent manner. The notion attracted the attention of government and the President of the Board of Trade, Sydney Buxton, set about creating a 'business court' under the chairmanship of George Askwith who received a knighthood and was given the title of Comptroller-General of the Labour Department of the Board of Trade and Chief Industrial Commissioner. The new body was named the Industrial Council and was made up of twenty-six members – thirteen each from the employers and the unions. Among the employers' representatives were Macara himself together with G. H. Claughton (chairman of the London and North Western Railway) and Sir T. Ratcliffe Ellis (secretary of the Lancashire and Cheshire Coalowners Association) both of whom were to serve subsequently on the Whitley Committee during the First World War. Among the union representatives were Thomas Burt, Arthur Henderson, John Hodge and J. R. Clynes, all of whom were MPs. Clynes, organizing secretary of the NUGGL, was also to serve on the Whitley Committee.

From its inception the Industrial Council was lacking both in power and influence. Notwithstanding its distinguished membership it failed to gain the confidence of industry at large and, in particular, those sections which were not directly represented among its members. The view was firmly rooted that, although conciliation might be useful in breaking a deadlock, only those directly involved in an industry could resolve an industrial dispute. Outsiders such as Askwith might well have a role to play in a crisis but negotiators were unwilling to make use of the Industrial Council which they saw as bearing the taint of government interference. When a dispute broke out in the cotton industry Sir Charles Macara himself led the employers in imposing a lockout without referring the matter to the Council, thereby damaging his own case for its creation. The Industrial Council was deemed a failure and the government allowed it to lapse in 1913. A precedent had, however, been set and, as will be seen, similar bodies were to emerge in the form of the Committee on Production, the Arbitration Tribunals and the Industrial Court. Perhaps its main achievement, however, was, as Charles has observed, in producing a report on industrial agreements which helped consolidate moderate opinion 'behind the belief that the main immediate task was to give the maximum possible encouragement to collective bargaining and the trade unionism on which it depended'.[13]

Notes and references

The place of publication is London unless stated otherwise.

1. The Junta was the name coined by Sidney and Beatrice Webb for the small group of London-based trade union leaders who were active in pursuing legislative reforms during the 1860s and early 1870s. As well as Robert Applegarth the group included William Allan of the Engineers, Daniel Guile of the Ironfounders, Edwin Coulson of the London Order of Bricklayers and George Odger, a member of the skilled union of ladies shoe makers and a leading working-class Radical. See Chapter 5 of the Webbs' *History of Trade Unionism*, 1912.
2. Tenth Report of the Commissioners appointed to inquire into the Organization and Rules of Trades Unions and other associations, 28 July 1868 page 76, para. 19,375.
3. *A History of Political Thought*, Hinsdale Illinois, 1973.
4. *The Diary of Beatrice Webb* Volume I 1873–1892, MacKenzie N. and J. (eds) 1982.
5. *A History of British Trade Unionism*, Harmondsworth 1976 edition.
6. 'Trade Unions and the Development of Independent Labour Politics 1889–1906' in Pimlott B. and Cook C. (eds.) *Trade Unions in British Politics*, 1982.
7. *Labour and Socialism: A History of the British Labour Movement 1867–1974*, Brighton 1983.
8. *The Origins of Trade Union Power*, Oxford 1983.
9. Quoted in Cambridge House Bulletins. Trade Boards 1 Serial No 26, 24 July 1922.
10. *Our Partnership*, Cambridge 1975 edition.
11. *The State and the Trade Unions* 1976.
12. *Industrial Problems and Disputes* 1920.
13. *The Development of Industrial Relations in Britain 1911–1939*, 1973.

Chapter 3

The Impact of War

Industrial unrest continued right up to the outbreak of war on 4 August 1914. The opening of hostilities had a sobering effect, however, on employers and unions alike. As Lord Amulree observed 'it appeared that nothing could save many industries from hopeless collapse'. In an effort to limit the damage to industry and avoid widespread unemployment the trade union movement called an 'industrial truce' and the level of strike activity was dramatically reduced. In the event, however, the rapid recruitment of men for the army, coupled with the expanding production of war material, led to dire labour shortages in many areas of industry. In particular the shortage of skilled men soon began to place limitations on the country's capacity to produce sufficient quantities of munitions to meet the requirements of the army as it settled into the long war of attrition on the Western Front. On 21 December 1914 the 'Shell Conference' was convened and the Board of Trade proposed that industrial disputes in engineering should, for the duration of the war, be settled without recourse to strikes or lockouts and also that the engineering unions should abandon restrictive practices and accept dilution. These proposals, calculated to increase production by reducing the number of disruptive stoppages and permitting restructuring of the labour process so as to increase the deployment of unskilled workers, were supported by the War Office and the Admiralty. They also received the support of government and, in February 1915, Prime

Minister Askwith appointed the Committee on Production in Engineering and Shipbuilding Establishments charged with negotiating productivity improvements with employers and trade unions in the munitions industries during the period of emergency caused by the war. The Committee was made up of Sir George Askwith, representing the Board of Trade; Sir Francis Hopwood, representing the Admiralty; and Sir George Gibb, representing the War Office. H. J. Wilson, formerly registrar of the Industrial Council, became secretary of the Committee which began work immediately on its task holding meetings with employers associations and trade unions and issuing reports on such matters as time-keeping, demarcation and the appropriate use of semi-skilled and unskilled labour.

Labour shortages gave unprecedented bargaining power to workers and, as manufacturers' profits soared, wage demands increased and were backed by unofficial strikes. Whereas in January 1915 only ten disputes were known to the Labour Department of the Board of Trade, by February the figure had increased to forty-seven and by March it was seventy-four. The pressure of strike action prompted the Committee on Production to recommend that the government take action to prevent all stoppages on official war work caused by strikes or lockouts. Further, where agreement could not be reached by the parties to a dispute, the Committee recommended that the matter be referred to an impartial tribunal for arbitration. Following these recommendations it became government policy to seek the co-operation of the trade union leadership in finding a means of avoiding strikes by the use of compulsory arbitration and also to persuade the unions to lift restrictions on output by accepting dilution. Both of these issues were highly contentious and likely to generate hostility among union leaders and rank and file members alike. In an effort to obtain a voluntary agreement the Chancellor of the Exchequer, Lloyd George, invited the Parliamentary Committee of the TUC, together with the leaders of thirty-six unions involved in war production, to a conference at the Treasury. He succeeded in persuading the bulk of the unions to accept the Committee on Production's recommendations, although the coalminers refused to agree and the engineers (in the shape of the ASE) held out for better terms and taxation of company profits. This agreement, or concordat (known as the Treasury Agreement), was a final attempt to gain trade union co-operation by exhortation. The government crisis of May 1915, springing largely from press accusations concerning government complacency over the war effort, led to the establishment of the first wartime coalition and the creation of the Ministry of Munitions. Lloyd George became Minister of Munitions and immediately brought forward legislative proposals outlawing strikes and lockouts that went much further than the vague commitments contained in the Treasury Agreement. Under the Munitions of War Act of 1915 the trade unions were required to forego the right to strike, accept dilution and recognise compulsory arbitration. Further, by Royal Proclamation, prohibition of strikes could be extended beyond munitions work to any branch of industry. The Act was only partially successful in restraining industrial action and, indeed, generated grievances by introducing a system of leaving certificates without which workers could not leave the munitions industry and which smacked of industrial conscription. During 1915 nearly 3 million working days were lost through strike action and almost 2.5 million were lost in 1916. These figures were, of course, modest by pre-war standards (in 1913 and 1914 the number of days lost was closer to 10 million per annum) but nevertheless the number of strikes in crucial industries such as engineering, shipbuilding and coalmining placed a severe strain on the war effort.

Despite growing evidence of tension between the official leaderships and the rank and file members, trade union policy supported the war effort and as the war continued union and Labour leaders became directly involved in government. Arthur Henderson, leader of the Labour Party for the duration of the war, received a Cabinet post in the 1915 coalition, becoming President of the Board of Education and advisor on labour problems. When Lloyd George succeeded Askwith as Prime Minister in 1916 he included Henderson in his War Cabinet of five. John Hodge of the Steel Smelters became the inaugural Minister of Labour; George Barnes of the ASE became Minister of Pensions; and J. R. Clynes became Food Controller. In addition to direct participation in government the unions were also given a share in the control of industry with representation on such bodies as the Cotton and Wool Control Boards.[1] The collaboration of the trade union leadership with government imposed a growing strain on the unions' coherence as institutions. Trade union leaders' close association with governmental measures rendered them automatically suspect to the bulk of the rank and file membership. Such measures as dilution and the acceptance of compulsory arbitration were contrary to orthodox trade union policy and the union leaders were increasingly accused of having become parties to reaction. Union leaders had already been under attack from militant elements among their memberships in the years preceding the war. The heightening mood of militancy which developed as the war progressed led to the emergence of unofficial leaders and brought the shop stewards' movement into prominence. Labour shortage and the problems arising from attempts to impose dilution enhanced the power of shop stewards and, in some cases, led to a direct challenge to the national trade union organizations as the stewards formed their own works committees and established links with colleagues in other workshops. The potential of the shop stewards' movement was evidenced by the unofficial strikes on the Clyde in February 1915 and much of the industrial unrest throughout the war was orchestrated by unofficial leaders. Discontent with the trade union leaderships came to a head in the wave of strikes during 1917 which resulted in the loss of 6 million working days and prompted the government to establish the Commission of Inquiry into Industrial Unrest under the chairmanship of George Barnes.

In May 1915 the Committee on Production became the central arbitration tribunal and made hundreds of awards throughout the duration of the war. The overall effect of the Committee's work was to encourage industry-wide pay agreements and stimulate the further development of industry-wide organizations of unions and employers. Trade unions received official encouragement and membership grew rapidly from a little over 4 million in 1914 to more than 6.5 million in 1918. Membership continued to increase during the brief boom which followed the war and peaked at 8.3 million in 1920.[2] Much of this growth was to prove highly perishable and numbers were rapidly dissipated during the recession years of the early 1920s. Similarly the bulk of the Committee on Production's interventions in the field of pay determination were problematical. Many of their awards were merely temporary war bonuses and, again and again, their findings carried the following caveat: 'the advance to be regarded as war wages, and recognised as due to and dependent on the existence of the abnormal conditions now prevailing in consequence of the war.'[3] At the war's end the unions were faced with defending their members' financial gains whilst attempting to obtain the restoration of historic working practices which had been suspended for the duration of the war. The employers, on the other hand, were eager to resist the restoration of such practices and desired to damp down the level of wages. The government, recognising the disruptive possibilities of the situation, responded by implementing a series of special measures. The emphasis of the government's industrial training schemes, for example, was shifted away from the rapid throughput of semi-skilled operatives to the provision of skill training for returning service personnel both able-bodied and disabled. The Wages (Temporary Regulation) Act of November 1918 repealed the legal provisions prohibiting strikes and lockouts, compulsory arbitration was discontinued and an Interim Court of Arbitration established which became the Industrial Court in 1919. In an effort to prevent a rapid reduction in wages the standard rates in operation at the date of the armistice were continued for six months as legally binding minima, and this provision was subsequently extended for a similar period. Further, under the Trade Boards Act of 1918, a rapid expansion of the trade boards system was undertaken in an attempt to place a safety net under wage rates. In the event none of these measures proved adequate to resist the social and economic dislocation which followed the cessation of hostilities. A brief economic boom, accompanied by serious industrial unrest, was followed by recession, a series of defensive strikes and widespread unemployment.

The Whitley reports

The Committee on Relations between Employers and Employed (usually referred to as the Whitley Committee after its chairman, J. H. Whitley) was originally appointed as a sub-committee of the first Cabinet Committee on Reconstruction established in March 1916. It continued its work as a sub-committee of the second Reconstruction Committee, set up by Lloyd George in March 1917, and completed its task under the auspices of the Ministry of Reconstruction when it was created in August 1917. The impulse for convening the Whitley Committee sprang from the unique industrial circumstances of the First World War. During the early months of 1916 the Cabinet Committee on Reconstruction examined several problems which had arisen as a result of the various government measures affecting industrial organization and policy, which had been taken since August 1914. Firstly, the war situation and the operation of the Munitions of War Act had led to the suspension of the normal machinery of collective bargaining over a wide field of industry. Secondly, in the event of the war being won (or at least ended) it was realised that administrative machinery would be required in order to facilitate an orderly cessation of government control of industry, the restoration of trade union practices, demobilisation of the armed forces and a return to peacetime conditions. Finally, there was a general recognition of the need to build on the industrial relations system which had evolved since 1914 and not to return to the industrial unrest which had blighted the immediate pre-war years.[4]

The Whitley Committee was appointed in October 1916 with the following terms of reference:

(1) To make and consider suggestions for securing a permanent improvement in the relations between employers and workmen.
(2) To recommend means for securing that industrial conditions affecting the relations between employers and workmen should be systematically reviewed by those concerned with a view to improving conditions in the future.[5]

The Committee held its first meeting on 9 November 1916 and continued to meet at regular intervals until July 1918. At an early stage it was agreed that the best approach to the Committee's work would be to identify broad areas of debate such as 'the means of enlisting the co-operation of labour on the constructive side of industry'; the 'study of existing organizations for joint and continuous consideration of trade matters' and the 'means by which such organizations could be perfected'; and 'the functions, if any, that the State could perform to assist improvement'.[6] On these and other issues the members of the Committee were invited to submit memoranda for general consideration and responses were also invited from interested individuals and organizations. The Board of Trade, for example, submitted evidence on the operation of the trade boards system. However, as Lord Amulree observed, the Whitley Committee, 'unlike most of those that had previously inquired into labour matters heard comparatively few witnesses. Most of the members had the essential facts within their own knowledge'.[7]

The members of the Committee were variously experienced. J. H. Whitley, a Liberal MP and owner of a firm of cotton spinners in Halifax, was not himself an industrial relations specialist but an experienced chairman of committees who went on to become Speaker of the House of Commons and chairman of the Board of Governors of the BBC. Although he disclaimed credit for the industrial relations system which came to bear his name (viz. Whitleyism) he continued publicly to advocate it until his death in 1935. The trade union representatives included Robert Smillie, a founder member of the ILP and president of the Miners' Federation from 1912 to 1921, and J. R. Clynes of the NUGGL who had been a Labour MP since 1906 and had served on the Industrial Council. The remaining two trade unionists were F. S. Button, a member of the executive of the ASE from 1913 to 1917 and a member of the Committee on Production, and Susan Lawrence a LCC Councillor and executive committee member of the Women's Trade Union League who later became a Labour MP. The leading employers' representative was Sir Allan Smith of the Engineering Employers Federation, who had been at the centre of the campaign to obtain the suspension of workshop custom and practice in the engineering industry, and became the architect of the National Confederation of Employers' Organizations in 1919. Both the remaining employers representatives, Sir George Claughton and Sir Thomas Ratcliffe Ellis, were former members of the Industrial Council. In addition to trade union and employers representatives the Committee also had a number of independent members. They included the author and radical J. A. Hobson; S. J. Chapman, an authority on industrial relations in the cotton industry; Mona Wilson, a social investigator and associate of Mary Macarthur; and J. J. Mallon, the secretary of the National Anti-Sweating League. The Committee secretaries were Arthur Greenwood, who went on to pursue a political career and, in the role of Deputy Leader of the Labour Party, became a member of Churchill's War Cabinet in 1940 and H. J. Wilson, who had been the registrar of the Industrial Court, was secretary of the Committee on Production and later became Permanent Secretary at the Ministry of Labour. Broadly speaking all the members of the Whitley Committee, together with the joint secretaries, were sympathetic to the progressive view of industrial relations pioneered by the Labour Department of the Board of Trade and advocated in the single report of the Industrial Council. Even such disparate figures as Smillie and Smith were willing to advocate collaboration between capital and labour. The rationale for such collaboration was, however, firmly rooted in the specific circumstances of the war and did not long survive the cessation of hostilities.

The Whitley Committee produced a total of five reports beginning with the Interim Report of March 1917. It was this document which introduced the basic structure of Whitleyism. Each industry was to establish a national, standing, joint council consisting of representatives of trade unions and employers associations with similar bodies to be created at district level. These two tiers were to be underpinned by joint works committees so that a three-fold structure would exist ranging from the workshop floor to national level. The Committee assumed that such a system would only be possible where workers and employers were 'well organized' – that is highly unionised and possessing representative employers' associations. In effect this meant a relatively small group of major industries including

coalmining, shipbuilding and textiles where collective bargaining
was already well established. In the event the major industries
rejected the proposals and Whitleyism made its greatest impact
in municipal and government employment. In its second report
published in March 1918 the Committee turned its attention
to those industries where collective bargaining was weak and
recommended the extension of the trade boards system. A third
report examined the role of the works committees that had been
established during the war and identified such committees as
providing the broad base of their proposed structure – 'an
essential means by which alone the principles of the Whitley
Scheme can be successfully carried through the whole industrial
field and brought home to industrial workers'.[8] The works
committee system failed to develop even where Whitleyism
became the favoured form of industrial relations and the system
became a 'top-down' approach offering little direct participation
to rank and file trade union members or workers. The Committee
considered that the proposals contained in its first three reports
would provide a structure of industrial relations capable of
maintaining a permanent improvement in the relations between
employers and workers. The scheme of interlocking committees,
meeting on a regular basis, was seen as offering the means for
continuous review of conditions in a specific industry and
obviating conflict through a process of institutionalised dialogue.
The Committee were, however, aware that some differences
might prove to be insoluble within an industry's own joint
structure. Thus in their fourth report they recommended 'the
establishment of a small Standing Arbitration Council, on the
lines of the . . . Committee on Production, to deal with cases
where the parties . . . failed to come to an agreement'.[9] The
Committee resisted the temptation to advocate a continuation of
compulsory arbitration, which they considered had not worked
well during the war, taking the view that the fulfilment of
industrial agreements is best based on moral obligation and
mutual consent rather than legal compulsion.[10] The Whitley
Committee presented its final report in July 1918 noting that,
since its establishment, the Ministry of Labour and the Ministry
of Reconstruction had been created and numerous joint industrial
councils set up on the basis of the proposals contained in the

Interim Report. Fearing overlap with these new bodies, and considering its task completed, the Committee stated its desire to be excused from further work and was allowed by the government to lapse.

The implementation of policy

By the end of September 1917 the War Cabinet were aware that the response of the trade unions and employers to the Interim Report of the Whitley Committee was generally favourable although it was obvious that the bulk of the country's major industries were unlikely to participate in the scheme. The War Cabinet endorsed the proposals in early September and their implementation was entrusted to the Ministry of Labour operating under the auspices of the Ministry of Reconstruction. The Ministry of Labour was established by Lloyd George in December 1916 as one of the conditions for gaining the political support of the Labour Party. It was created out of the semi-autonomous Labour Department of the Board of Trade and Sir David Shackleton became its Permanent Secretary. Shackleton was a former cotton operative and president of the Weavers' Amalgamation who had been elected Labour MP for Clitheroe in 1902. In 1910 he had abandoned his political career to become labour adviser to the Home Office. Lloyd George originally intended that the first Minister of Labour should be the railwaymen's leader J. H. Thomas, but Thomas refused the post when he learned that Arthur Henderson had been asked to join the War Cabinet as Labour's representative. Instead, the job went to John Hodge the founder, and for thirty years the leader, of the Steel Smelters' union. Hodge soon encountered problems with his civil servants especially William Beveridge and Sir George Askwith both of whom felt a prior claim on the post of Permanent Secretary of the new Ministry. It was Hodge who appointed Shackleton; insisting that Shackleton receive a knighthood in order that he might meet Askwith on terms of equality. Beveridge went as far as to suggest to Hodge that he should become joint Permanent Secretary and was quickly drafted to the Ministry of Food where he remained until 1919.[11] Askwith, however, remained at the Ministry of Labour becoming involved in disputes both with other departments and his own Minister. Askwith was rightly frustrated at the lack of co-ordination of labour matters which developed under the Lloyd George coalition. Ultimately his nuisance value outweighed his usefulness and, following the election of December 1918, the new Minister of Labour, Sir Robert Horne, insisted that Askwith be dismissed. Askwith was forced to resign and grudgingly rewarded for his services with a peerage. In July 1919 he wrote a famous letter to *The Times* in which he characterised Lloyd George's interventions in industrial disputes as 'a degradation of government'.[12] Hodge was a failure at the Ministry of Labour and was moved to the Ministry of Pensions in August 1917. He was replaced by George Roberts who, like both Hodge and Shackleton, was a right-wing trade unionist and leader of the Typographical Association. By the time Roberts became Minister some of the internecine strife had abated but the Ministry had failed to resolve its quarrels with other departments or gain central control of manpower policy. Thus the Department of National Service held responsibility for the distribution of manpower while the labour department of the Ministry of Munitions (established by Llewellyn Smith who opposed the creation of the Ministry of Labour, seeing it as merely a partisan creature of the trade unions) remained autonomous. Further, the War Office, the Admiralty and the Board of Trade, through the Coal Controller and the Railway Executive Committee all retained autonomy in industrial relations matters. In this situation the Ministry of Labour's role was destined to be advisory rather than executive.

With the departure of Beveridge, Shackleton developed the role of chief labour advisor to the government in competition with Askwith and Henderson. A former colleague of Shackleton's at the Home Office, Harold Butler, took responsibility for the day to day running of the Ministry and also the development of long-term policy. Butler established the Joint Industrial Councils Division to promote the creation of Whitley Councils, placing it under the control of the economist Henry Clay and including J. J. Mallon among its staff. In his memoirs Butler speaks of 'the still small voice' of the infant Ministry[13] and Lowe has depicted the prestige of the Ministry of Labour from 1916 to 1919 as negligible.[14] The inherent weakness of the Ministry was, however, mitigated in August 1917 when Lloyd George established the Ministry of Reconstruction. The Minister of Reconstruction, Dr Christopher Addison, was one of Lloyd George's principal supporters and had succeeded him at the Ministry of Munitions. Addison was given powers to appoint committees and co-ordinate policies relating to reconstruction but the Ministry's first priority was to make provision for the demobilisation of the army and to deal with the displacement of munitions and other war workers when hostilities ceased. Addison devoted his first public speech as Minister to the advocacy of Whitley Councils and he also inaugurated the Industrial Reconstruction Council to propagate knowledge of the recommendations contained in the Whitley Committee's Interim Report. Early in 1918 the Ministry felt justified in claiming that 'the reception given to the Whitley Committee's Report by rival schools of opinion is the most promising development, so far, in connection with Reconstruction plans'.[15]

By October 1917 many of the Ministry of Labour's initial problems had been solved and the prestige of Addison was available to promote the task of implementing the Whitley proposals. On 20 October George Roberts sent a circular letter to the leading employers' associations and trade unions, informing them that the War Cabinet had adopted the recommendations contained in the Interim Report as a central plank in their policy of industrial reconstruction. Roberts' letter showed a decisive shift of emphasis away from merely improving the relations between employers and employed to finding a suitable mechanism for coping with the manpower problems likely to emerge in the aftermath of the war. Thus 'the problems of the period of transition and reconstruction' following the war and 'the task of rebuilding the social and economic fabric on a broader and surer foundation will be rendered much easier if in the organized trades there exist representative bodies' to which 'questions of difficulty' such as 'demobilisation of the Forces, the resettlement of munitions workers in civil industries, apprenticeship (especially where interrupted by war services), the training and employment of disabled soldiers, and the control of raw materials can be referred'.[16] The first Whitley Council was established (in the pottery industry) in January 1918 and this was followed by the building industry in May of that year. By July 1919 the number of Councils had risen to forty-one and, at the end of 1921, the figure stood at seventy-three with 150 district councils and 1,000 works committees in existence. Between 1918 and 1921 the Ministry of Labour, through its Joint Industrial Councils Division, was active in promoting the establishment of Whitley Councils, convening representative conferences and advising on constitutional issues. However, by 1921 enthusiasm for Whitleyism was waning and fifteen of the Whitley Councils had already ceased to function. The Ministry of Reconstruction was abolished in June 1919 and although the Ministry of Labour survived, its budget was halved following the Geddes Report on public expenditure. Between 1921 and 1930 only three national Whitley Councils were formed whilst a total of thirty ceased to function.[17] Direct government support for Whitleyism ended in the rapidly changing circumstances of the post-war period and was not restored until the Second World War.

The extension of trade board protection

The First World War drastically redefined the problem of low pay. Regulation of wages under the Munitions of War Acts, labour shortages and the generally enhanced role of labour brushed aside many of the old arguments relating to state intervention in matters of pay and conditions. However, as the war began to draw to a close, fears were expressed concerning the possible dislocation of industry in the immediate post-war period and the likely adverse effects of this on vulnerable members of the labour force. As the Ministry of Labour saw the situation in 1918, there was 'reason to fear that the problem of inadequate wages for unskilled and unorganized workers, particularly women, may be rendered exceptionally acute (and) competition for employment may reduce wages to an unduly low level, unless precautionary measures are taken'.[18] In 1917 the Women's Employment Committee of the Ministry of Reconstruction recommended that the trade boards system be extended to provide widespread protection for women workers. Three members of this Committee (Susan Lawrence, Mona Wilson and J. J. Mallon) were also members of the Whitley Committee and veteran campaigners for statutory minimum rates of pay. Not surprisingly, perhaps, the Whitley Commissioners in their second report recommended the extension of the trade boards system as part of a wider strategy aimed at bringing about improved relations between employers and employed. Their recommendation was accepted by government and given legislative form in the Trade Boards Act 1918 which Bayliss has characterised as the major achievement of the Whitley Committee[19]. Under the 1918 Act responsibility for administering the extended trade boards system was transferred from the Board of Trade to the Ministry of Labour, and the 1909 Act amended in three principal respects. Firstly, the Minister of Labour was empowered to apply the Act to new trades without confirmation by Parliament. Secondly, the Minister could do so not merely on the basis of exceptionally low rates of pay but on the basis of inadequate organization of workers and employers to enable effective collective bargaining to take place. Thirdly, the boards were empowered to fix not just time and piece rates but also overtime and guaranteed time rates. In the aftermath of the passing of the 1918 Act a rapid increase in the number of trade boards occurred and, by the end of 1921, there were sixty-three boards in existence covering some three million workers.

The provisions of the 1918 Act took the trade boards system far beyond the original intention of the 1909 legislation. Thus it did not merely deal with trades where 'sweating' on the House of Lords definition of 1890 was occurring, but also industries where collective organization was poor. Significantly, whereas the basis of the 1909 Act had been an attempt to achieve social justice, the basis of the 1918 Act was quite clearly governmental expediency aimed at avoiding labour unrest. Not surprisingly, as the brief post-war boom gave way to recession, employers began a campaign for repeal of the 1918 Act which resulted in the appointment of the Cave Committee, charged with examining the effects of the Trade Boards Acts. In their report, published in 1922, the Committee grouped the major charges made by the employers' representatives under five headings:

(a)   that the high level of minimum rates fixed by the trade boards, together with the general lack of differentiation to meet local conditions, caused unemployment by over-pricing labour;

(b)   that the rates fixed, by overpricing labour, had assisted foreign producers at the cost of home traders;

(c)   that the rates fixed for juvenile workers had interfered with the recruitment and training of young people, thereby jeopardising the future of the trade;

(d)   that too many boards had been created causing problems of demarcation and generating friction in industry;

(e)   that the amount of time required to achieve revision of pay rates rendered it impossible to modify wages in line with changes in the cost of living.

The Committee did not state specifically to what extent any of the employers' charges were proven and couched their conclusions in general terms only. They gave their opinion that the trade boards system had accomplished valuable work in substantially improving the conditions of workers in the unorganized trades, particularly those of women, and in abolishing 'sweating'. Further, the system had given protection to good employers, who were willing and able to pay a reasonable rate of pay, from unscrupulous competitors prepared to take unfair advantage of their workers. Indeed, the Committee were willing to concede that the system had improved industrial relations and acted as a stimulus to improve working methods. On the other hand, they accepted, with only slight reserve, the view that the operation of some of the trade boards had contributed to trade depression and unemployment. The Committee opposed the total repeal of the Acts, however, on the basis that it would lead to the rapid return of 'sweating'. Instead, they proposed a restoration of the system to that embodied in the 1909 Act (i.e. the limitation of state interference with wages to situations where cases of gross oppression of individuals and injury to national health were observed).[20] The Conservative Government accepted this proposal and, in 1923, set about preparing legislation intended to substantially reduce the scope of the trade boards.

The opposition of the labour movement to the Committee's proposal was predictable. At the 1922 TUC, Margaret Bondfield moved a motion condemning the Cave Report and its recommendations. She noted that the government was not operating the 1918 Act properly and had recently cut the Ministry of Labour inspectorate. A motion of condemnation was carried and it became TUC policy to oppose the Cave recommendations.[21] Similarly, the 1923 Labour Party Conference supported a motion expressing 'its strong desire for the continuance of the trade boards system . . . and its emphatic disapproval of those provisions of the Trade Boards Bill now before Parliament'.[22] When Labour formed a minority government in January 1924 it abandoned the proposed legislation and announced its intention of extending the trade boards system to more industries. The new government set about improving enforcement and extending the system to the distributive trades, where only milk distribution was currently covered.[23] However, the return of the Conservatives in November 1924, ended the possibility of substantially extending the number of trade boards. In the event, the new government decided against fresh legislation and announced that they would administer the system according to the spirit of the Cave Report.[24] That is, avoidance of the worst aspects of 'sweating' but little more. Although the Labour Government of 1929 succeeded in bringing about a partial revival of the system, substantial extension of trade board protection did not take place until the Second World War.

The Industrial Court

The Industrial Courts Act 1919 gave the Minister of Labour powers of conciliation similar to those which were given to the Board of Trade under the 1896 Act. It also introduced two new features in the form of a permanent Industrial Court and a system of Courts of Inquiry. The draft Bill for the Industrial Courts Act differed from the Whitley Committee's proposals by making arbitration awards legally binding for a period of four months. During September 1919 the Minister of Labour, Sir Robert Horne, attempted to persuade the trade unions, via the TUC Parliamentary Committee, to accept this modification which would have made it illegal for trade unions to give strike pay during the 'cooling-off' period. The TUC claimed that this provision would infringe the unions' rights under the Trade Disputes Act, and the provisions for legal compulsion were ultimately deleted from the final Bill which became the Industrial Courts Act on 20 November 1919.[25] The Industrial Court was not a court in the conventional sense but a tribunal with an independent, permanent president (and three chairmen) and panels of employer and trade union representatives, all appointed by the Minister of Labour. The first president, Sir William Mackenzie (later Lord Amulree) hoped that the Court would be used to establish a body of case law similar to the English Common Law and capable of being applied in industrial disputes. Disputes could only be referred to the Industrial Court by the Minister of Labour with the consent of both parties, and when a particular industry's internal procedures had been exhausted.

In addition to a permanent court of arbitration the 1919 Act extended the 1896 provisions so as to give the Minister of Labour powers of conciliation, in threatened as well as existing disputes, by providing for the appointment of Courts of Inquiry. These were used sparingly during the inter-war period with the exception of 1924 when Tom Shaw, Minister of Labour in the first Labour Government, adopted a policy of 'letting the public know the facts'.[26] The announcement of this policy encouraged the trade unions to demand Courts of Inquiry for tactical purposes thereby impairing the use of the established machinery of collective bargaining. The number of cases dealt with under the 1896 and 1919 Acts declined during the inter-war period, falling from over 900 in 1920 to 52 in 1933 and only increasing with the economic recovery of the late 1930s. Administration of the 1896 and 1919 Acts was carried out by a team of Ministry of Labour officials including a Chief Conciliation Officer stationed in each major industrial region. These officials were charged with encouraging industrial conciliation in their specific areas and also providing the Ministry with intelligence concerning situations which might lead to an industrial dispute. During the inter-war period the Ministry of Labour took over the independent advisory role in industrial relations which had been pioneered by Llewellyn Smith at the Labour Department of the Board of Trade.

Notes and references

1. MacDonald D. *The State and the Trade Unions*, 1976.
2. Wrigley C. 'Trade Unions and Politics in the First World War' in Pimlott B. and Cook C. (eds.) *Trade Unions in British Politics*, 1982.
3. Committee on Production: Findings March 1915 to May 1917.
4. Report on the Establishment and Progress of Joint Industrial Councils, 1923.
5. Cmd. 8606 Interim Report on Joint Standing Industrial Councils, 1917.
6. Report on the Establishment etc. op. cit.
7. *Industrial Arbitration in Great Britain*, 1929.
8. Report on the Establishment etc. op. cit.
9. Cmd. 9153 Committee on Relations Between Employers and Employed, Final Report, 1918.
10. Cmd. 9099 Committee on Relations Between Employers and Employed, Report on Conciliation and Arbitration, 1918.
11. Harris J. *William Beveridge: A Biography*, Oxford 1977.
12. Wigham E. *Strikes and the Government 1893–1981*, 1982.
13. *Confident Morning*, 1950.
14. 'The Ministry of Labour 1916–1919: A Still Small Voice?' in Burk K. (ed.) *War and the State*, 1982.
15. Reconstruction Problems No. 1: The Aims of Reconstruction, Ministry of Reconstruction, 1918.
16. Industrial Report No. 1: Industrial Councils, Ministry of Labour, 1918.
17. Seymour, J. *The Whitley Council Scheme*, 1932.
18. Ministry of Labour Gazette Vol. XXVI January to December 1918.
19. Bayliss F. *British Wages Councils*, Oxford 1962.
20. Cmd. 1645 Report to the Minister of Labour of the Committee Appointed to Enquire into the Working and Effects of the Trade Boards Acts, 1922.
21. TUC Report, 1922.
22. Labour Party Annual Report, 1923.

23. 'Legislation for the Workers' Labour Publications Department, 1924.
24. Ministry of Labour Gazette Vol. XXXIII January to December 1925.
25. Sharp I. *Industrial Conciliation and Arbitration*, 1950.
26. *Labour and Industrial Peace*, Labour Publications Department, 1924.

Chapter 4

The Aftermath of War and the New Demands of Conflict

Fears of widespread unemployment and industrial dislocation at the war's end were not immediately borne out by events. Instead, a brief boom during 1919 absorbed those leaving the armed forces whilst the removal of women workers from industry progressed rapidly with three quarters of a million being dismissed between November 1918 and November 1919.[1] Indeed, the Ministry of Reconstruction's plans for an orderly management of the war's end proved inappropriate and were partially abandoned. Whilst the pattern of wartime controls were dismantled the Lloyd George coalition government played for time, alternately placating and confronting trade union militancy. Hinton has characterised the labour unrest which broke out during 1919 and 1920 as a working-class offensive and conceded that Lloyd George 'showed considerable understanding and tactical skill in handling and eventually breaking' it. By 1921 the government had succeeded in 'avoiding a general strike ... managed to abandon most of the apparatus of control, and go far towards depoliticising the sectional strikes and lockouts that accompanied the employer counter attack on inflated wartime wage rates'.[2] The post-war boom began to collapse during 1920 and the unions increasingly turned away from long term ambitions for such things as nationalisation and workers' control to short term demands for wage increases and, subsequently, resistance to wage cuts. The level of industrial unrest during the immediate post war years surpassed even that experienced during the period 1910 to

1914–35 million days were lost in 1919, 26 million in 1920, and almost 86 million in 1921. On average, during the years 1919 to 1922, 1,613,000 workers were involved in 1,075 stoppages causing the loss of 41,815,000 working days. In the previous worst period, the four years before the war, the annual average was 734,000 workers in 922 stoppages causing a loss of 17,681,000 days.[3]

Threats of industrial unrest prompted the Minister of Labour, Sir Robert Horne, to convene the National Industrial Conference which met at the Central Hall, Westminster on 27 February 1919. It brought together representatives from the bulk of British industry including 300 from the employers and 500 from the trade unions but excluding the ASE. The Minister opened the conference by declaring that the government was anxious to receive advice for meeting the difficulties in managing the transition from war to peace. Lloyd George also spoke and it was agreed to appoint a joint committee to consider means for improving the relationship between employers, trade unions and the state. This committee was led by Sir Allan Smith for the employers and Arthur Henderson for the trade unions, while J. J. Mallon represented the trade boards. Among the committee's early recommendations were proposals to establish a maximum normal working week of forty-eight hours (a reduction from the standard fifty-four hours); extend unemployment insurance; further extend the trade boards system; and for the employers to fully recognise the trade unions. Several of these proposals were put into effect – unemployment insurance was extended, as was the trade boards system and working hours were reduced to forty-eight hours for some 7 million workers. A further recommendation to establish a permanent National Industrial Council consisting of 400 members representing the two sides of industry and presided over by the Ministry of Labour was not, however, proceeded with. In the event industrial turbulence soured the relationship between the two sides of industry and the Conference lapsed when the trade union representatives walked out in disgust at what they saw as the negative attitude of the employers. It was to be several years before a further attempt was made to establish a system of national co-operation between employers and trade unions when, in the aftermath of the General

Strike, the Mond–Turner talks took place in 1928–29.

Economic recession began in 1920 and had its most severe impact on the war expanded industries. Shipbuilding, iron and steel, and engineering all suffered rapid decline as did coalmining and cotton textiles, both of which were damaged by the collapse of the export trade. After a brief recovery in 1924 Britain's economy remained in what Pigou described as the doldrums for the remainder of the 1920s with a hard core of 1 million unemployed. As recession deepened trade union membership declined, falling from 8.3 million (or 45 per cent of the workforce) in 1920 to a low of under 4.4 million (or 23 per cent of the workforce) in 1933. Although there was a slow recovery during the late 1930s, by 1938 membership had only increased to a little over 6 million (or 30 per cent of the workforce).[4] One effect of the recession on collective bargaining was the emergence of sliding scale agreements based on changes in the cost of living index calculated by the Board of Trade. By the late 1920s some 2.5 million workers were covered by such agreements including, for example, tramway workers and those employed in the gas, water and electricity supply industries. Although these agreements were negotiated on the basis that wage levels could fluctuate up or down, recession led to rapid downward pressure on pay as the Board of Trade index fell from 152 in 1920 to 119 in 1921, 84 in 1922 and 69 in 1923. Reductions negotiated by sliding scale agreements brought about cuts in money wages but tended to preserve gains made in real wages during the war. For several years, therefore, trade unions tended to defend sliding scale agreements but the brief improvement in the economic situation in 1924 caused the unions to become resistant to pay cuts in whatever form.

Britain's economy was badly affected by the worldwide recession which followed the crash on Wall Street in October 1929. Between 1929 and 1931 exports fell from £839 million to £461 million and, from 1931 to 1935, the number of unemployed remained above the 2 million mark. During the worst period of unemployment (the winter of 1932–33) almost 3 million people were out of work – a quarter of the insured population.[5] In the face of the crisis government turned belatedly to piecemeal protectionist measures in an attempt to reduce the vulnerability of the British economy. Recovery did occur after 1933 but it was slow and the percentage of unemployed workers was still over 10 per cent in 1939. The involvement of Britain in war with Germany, however, rapidly dissipated the industrial stagnation which had blighted the inter-war period and labour soon became the ultimate resource. From May 1940 the Labour Party took a leading role in Churchill's coalition government with Ernest Bevin becoming Minister of Labour and National Service. Bevin, architect of the TGWU and foremost trade union leader of the inter-war period, rapidly gained complete control over the allocation of manpower and, by dint of circumstances and personality, came to stand 'where no Cabinet Minister had previously done, rival to the Chancellor of the Exchequer himself'.[6]

The General Strike

The General Strike of 1926 arose out of economic difficulties in the coal industry and the determination of the coalowners to cut miners' pay. During the First World War the coal mines were placed under government control and the Miners Federation emerged from the war as the strongest trade union in the country. When, for example, the Whitley Committee's Interim Report was debated at the TUC in 1917 the Miners Federation delegate, Frank Hodges, dismissed its proposals with contempt saying 'you can never have permanent relations between employers and employed' and adding that the working men on the Committee (i.e. Clynes and Smillie) 'in their heart of hearts do not endorse these proposals'.[7] What the coalminers demanded was nationalisation of the pits under workers' control, not the opportunity of institutionalised negotiations with the coalowners. Interestingly, Hodges became secretary of the Miners Federation in 1918 but resigned in 1924 to enter Parliament as Civil Lord of the Admiralty in the first Labour Government. The union did not keep his job open nor, in spite of representations by Arthur Henderson, would they take him back and he was replaced by the militant A. J. Cook. In view of the sentiments he expressed in 1917 it is perhaps ironic that Hodges subsequently became the token labour member on the Central Electricity Board, when it was established by the Conservatives in 1926.

In January 1919 the Miners Federation held a special conference at Southport in order to formulate its post-war programme. This consisted of demands for a thirty per cent increase in wages, a six-hour working day and the nationalisation of all pits and minerals. Government remained in control of the coal industry and its response to the Southport programme was negative. The Miners Federation reacted by balloting its members on a national strike which resulted in a vote of six to one in favour of such action. Lloyd George then intervened directly by asking the miners to postpone the strike and participate in a commission to investigate the coal industry including questions of hours, wages and ownership. The miners agreed and Parliament established the Coal Industry Commission under the chairmanship of Sir John (later Lord) Sankey. The miners' interests were strongly represented on the Commission. In addition to Frank Hodges and Robert Smillie of the Miners Federation and Herbert Smith of the Yorkshire miners (who succeeded Smillie as president of the Miners Federation in 1922 and together with Cook played a prominent part in the General Strike), they also nominated three economists with Labour sympathies viz. Sidney Webb, R.H. Tawney and Sir Leo Chiozza Money. The remainder of the Commission was made up of three coalowners and three industrialists. The miners succeeded in turning the Commission 'into a grand jury, investigating the industry, cross-examining the royalty-owners and questioning their contribution to society and in general building up the case for nationalisation'.[8]

The Sankey Commission, as it became known, produced a series of reports between March and June 1919 which substantially supported in principle the miners' demands for improved pay and reduced hours although no consensus emerged on the issues. Briefly, the six miners' representatives advocated that the Southport programme be met in full whilst the coalowners and industrialists agreed that improvements were justified but differed on their scale. On the question of ownership there was agreement on the desirability of nationalising royalties but not

on the subject of ownership and control, even though Sir John
Sankey himself favoured nationalisation. There was thus no clear
majority report although the miners' representatives together
with Sir John Sankey commanded a majority of votes on the
Commission. Failure to produce a single, definitive report was
used by the government as an excuse for avoiding nationalisation.
Indeed, although the government did pass a Coal Mines Act in
1919 which enacted a seven hour day and also passed legislation
to limit profits and extend the period of government control,
it did not proceed with the nationalisation of royalties. In
effect the Sankey Commission provided the government with
a breathing space during a difficult period in industrial relations.
However, the subsequent cost of the ambitions and anxieties
that the Commission had aroused were to be high. As Mowat
has observed:

The bitterness and the troubles in the coal mines for the next seven – or
for that matter twenty-seven – years derived in great part from the
feeling of both miners and owners that they had been betrayed. The
miners, who had hoped for too much from the Commission, felt
tricked when they got nothing from it and the owners were furious
that the government had come so near to conceding nationalisation,
and having had a narrow escape they were more determined than ever
to stand firm in the future.[9]

On the eve of the First World War the coalminers became
associated with the railway and transport workers in a loose
federation for mutual support known as the Triple Industrial
Alliance. In theory at least, the grouping maintained some of
the notions of direct action and the advocacy of the general
strike which characterised syndicalism. As Symons observed
the Triple Alliance 'was, at least potentially, a very powerful
industrial instrument'.[10] Certainly it was taken seriously by
the government. When, for example, the Miners Federation
threatened strike action in 1919 the railway and transport
workers offered their support and the threat of such widespread
disruption prompted Lloyd George to establish the Sankey
Commission noted above. Early in 1921 the government revealed
that it would be ending control of the coalmines at the end of

March. The coalowners responded by announcing deep cuts in wages which, not surprisingly, were rejected by the miners. The coalowners then organized a lockout which resulted in the Triple Alliance calling a railway and transport strike to start on 12 April. The Lloyd George government reacted by declaring a State of Emergency and making open military preparations to resist civil disturbance, including the call-up of reservists and the posting of troops in some working-class areas. In the event conflict was avoided when Frank Hodges, almost unwittingly, accepted a wage settlement on a district, rather than national, basis. It was also obvious that the railway and transport workers were reluctant to commit themselves to action on behalf of the miners when their own sectional interests were not directly involved. Indeed, most prominent among those seeking a peaceful settlement to the dispute was the railwaymen's leader, J. H. Thomas. The failure of the unions to act in concert ended the Triple Alliance and convinced at least one of the leaders involved in the affair (i.e. Ernest Bevin) of the weakness of federations and alliances as opposed to full scale amalgamations.

The coalmining industry enjoyed a brief revival in 1923 when French troops occupied the Ruhr over Germany's failure to make reparation payments. The ensuing disruption boosted Britain's exports of coal and, in 1924, enabled the Miners Federation to negotiate a new national agreement with an increased minimum wage. Revival was, however, to be short lived. When Baldwin's Conservative Government decided to return to the gold standard the value of the pound was forced up with the effect that Britain's exports, including coal, became over-priced in world markets thereby reducing demand. As the export market for coal diminished and prices collapsed, the coalowners once again called for a reduction in miners' wages and an increase in working hours. These proposals were met with absolute rejection by the Miners Federation, now under the leadership of Herbert Smith and A. J. Cook, neither of whom were interested in compromise. Whereas the former leaders, Smillie and Hodges, had taken a pragmatic line and shown a willingness to negotiate, the stance of Smith and Cook was one of outright intransigence with coalowners, government and fellow trade unionists alike. As the crisis deepened the owners announced that the National Wages Agreement of 1924 would terminate on 31 July 1925 and be replaced by district level agreements coupled with wage reductions.

With the coalowners and the Miners Federation in deadlock other parties became increasingly involved in their dispute. The General Council of the TUC had been established in 1921 to replace the Parliamentary Committee and, by 1925, had obtained the authority to intervene in industrial disputes that involved large numbers of workers. The bulk of the General Council's work was delegated to sub-committees and a specific body – viz. the Special Industrial Committee (SIC) – was created to deal with the crisis in the coal industry. The SIC became the central trade union organization concerned with the events leading to the General Strike. In addition to the TUC the government became increasingly involved, with Prime Minister Baldwin doggedly resisting the miners' calls to alleviate the coal industry's problems by agreeing to pay a subsidy out of public funds. However, in the face of pressure from the TUC, and fearing the consequences of widespread industrial disruption, Baldwin did finally agree to subsidise the industry on condition that the miners' leaders participate in an inquiry into ways of improving productivity. The Miners Federation agreed to the proposal, strike action was averted, a subsidy of £23 million was paid by the government and a Royal Commission on the coal industry established under the chairmanship of Sir Herbert Samuel. While the Commission heard evidence the government used the opportunity to make detailed preparations for the major confrontation with the trade union movement which now seemed inevitable. When the Samuel Commission reported in March 1926 it offered nothing to alleviate the immediate problems in the industry. Once again there was support for the nationalisation of royalties and rationalisation of the industry was also advocated as a means of improving efficiency. On the question of wages, however, the Commission viewed the case for reductions as indisputable. It also opposed the continuation of the government's subsidy.

In his essay on the SIC Lovell has shown the deep divisions which existed in the trade union ranks on the eve of the General

Strike[11]. The most prominent individual on the SIC was J. H. Thomas who matched personal hostility for the miners' leaders with a conviction that there would need to be wage reductions and/or job losses before the immediate crisis in the coal industry could be resolved. Privately the miners' leaders also conceded that, if wages were to be maintained at their existing TUC levels, there would inevitably be substantial job losses. In their dealings with the coalowners, however, the Miners Federation maintained their uncompromising stance, flatly refusing to accept the Samuel Report or a new national agreement. The coal owners also rejected the Report and served notice that the miners' contracts would terminate on 30 April at which time a lockout would begin. When the General Council of the TUC met on 27 April to discuss the developing crisis it found that the SIC had no policy advice to give on the future of the coal industry and no contingency plans for use in the event of concerted strike action. Thus when a conference of union executives endorsed a General Council proposal to call a general strike in support of the miners on 3 May, the trade union movement was almost totally unprepared. The General Strike lasted only nine days and resulted in a total victory for the government. By 9 May the General Council were already convinced that, unless the miners were prepared to accept a reduction in wages, continuation of the strike would be useless. Although the TUC maintained that the strike was an industrial dispute rather than a constitutional issue, the government succeeded in depicting it as a direct attack on the democratically elected government. When the General Council met with Prime Minister Baldwin on 12 May it agreed to call off the strike and, as Wigham has observed, 'the surrender was unconditional'.[12] The coalminers fought on alone until

in November the men, beaten by cold and hunger, returned to work for longer hours and lower wages under district agreements and with no hope of reorganization of the industry. It was the longest, hardest and most bitter of all the long, hard and bitter struggles between the miners and the coal owners.[13]

The General Strike, or National Strike as the TUC preferred

to call it because only selected industries were called out, ended trade union calls for direct action. In the short term it also inflicted severe damage on the standing of the General Council and the labour movement at large. In 1927 the Trade Disputes and Trade Union Act was passed making sympathetic strikes and strikes directly and indirectly against the government illegal. It also introduced a 'contracting-in' system for the payment of trade union political funds, substantially prohibited picketing, restricted established civil servants from joining unions affiliated to the TUC and outlawed the closed shop in local government and other public authorities. The immediate effect of the 'contracting-in' system was to reduce the Labour Party's receipts from the trade unions by over 30 per cent. The reason for this was that members of affiliated unions who did not wish, or did not bother, to 'contract-in' could reduce their total subscriptions rather than support the Labour Party. The 1927 Act remained in operation for almost twenty years until it was finally repealed by the post-war Labour Government in 1946.

The advance of the Labour Party

The Labour Party did well out of the First World War. As we have seen several of its leading figures, and most prominently Arthur Henderson, gained ministerial experience in the coalition governments of Asquith and Lloyd George. Further, following Henderson's resignation from the War Cabinet in 1917, Sidney Webb and he prepared a new constitution for the party which both embraced socialist principles and broadened its electoral appeal. In the general election of December 1918 the Labour Party prospered, although the number of seats it won was not very much greater than in the pre-war period. More significant were the number of seats where Labour placed second ahead of the Liberal candidate. Divisions in the Liberal ranks after 1916 and the development of a mass electorate following the 1918 Reform Act worked together to give Labour the position of chief opposition party. As Renshaw has observed:

With 2,400,000 votes, or 22.7 per cent of those cast, Labour had clearly reached electoral take-off point, where a small increase in total votes would net a much larger increase in MPs. So it proved. Before Lloyd George's fall at the end of 1922, Labour had won fourteen by-elections and increased its vote almost everywhere. Within another twelve months Labour had won enough seats to form a government.[14]

After victory at the general election of 1918 Lloyd George had become a virtual prisoner of his Conservative allies. When he fell the Conservatives won power alone for the first time since 1902 and Bonar Law became Prime Minister, only to die six months later. His successor was Stanley Baldwin who favoured tariff reform (i.e. protection) and called a general election on the issue in December 1923. Although, when the votes were counted, their distribution was not greatly different from the year before; the results varied substantially with the Conservatives losing over ninety seats, the Liberals gaining forty and Labour fifty. No single party held a majority in Parliament; the Conservatives winning 258 seats, the Liberals 159 and Labour 191.[15] As the election had been fought on the issue of tariff reform and this had been rejected it was for the parties supporting free trade to form a government. In the event, and following the intervention of George V, Labour took office in January 1924 with Liberal support and Ramsay MacDonald became Prime Minister. Given the disposition of the parties it was assumed that MacDonald's ministry would be short lived and this proved to be the case with the Conservatives and Baldwin returning to power in November 1924. During its period of office the first Labour Government faced industrial unrest in several industries including the railways, the docks and building. Perhaps the most damaging strike for the government's reputation, however, was that involving London's passenger transport system. As we have noted in a previous chapter Labour's Minister of Labour was Tom Shaw, a self-educated cotton union leader. The Minister of Transport was the veteran trade union leader Harry Gosling who had only entered Parliament for the first time in 1923. Neither man was eager to confront their trade union colleagues. Nevertheless in the face of the stoppage of London's transport system Ramsay MacDonald threatened to use the Emergency

Powers Act which Labour had fiercely opposed when it was introduced by Lloyd George. Further the government accused the unions, and particularly Ernest Bevin, of disloyalty and working to undermine Labour's power. Bevin's response was forthright and noteworthy in terms of the relationship between future Labour governments and the trade unions. He said 'governments may come and governments may go but the workers' fight for betterment of conditions must go on all the time'.[16]

Labour returned to power in 1929, this time as the largest party in Parliament but still lacking an overall majority. Ramsay MacDonald was once again Prime Minister, while Margaret Bondfield gained the post of Minister of Labour and became the first woman Cabinet Minister. The central problem faced by the new government was that of unemployment. Unfortunately Labour lacked both the policies or the resolve to tackle the problem and, in any case, the government was soon over-whelmed by the effects of the depression. At the 1930 Labour Party Conference Oswald Mosley attempted to win support for a programme of increased public expenditure and reflation as a means of stimulating economic activity. A resolution supporting this policy was only narrowly defeated and Mosley resigned from the government to form the New Party and, subsequently, the British Union of Fascists. Instead of increasing public expenditure and pursuing reflation, however, the Chancellor of the Exchequer, Philip Snowden, adopted a package of defla-tionary measures including public spending cuts. In particular, following the financial crisis of August 1931, he proposed to reduce unemployment benefit and also to cut the pay of public employees including teachers, the police and the armed forces. The proposal to reduce unemployment benefit split the Cabinet and finally precipitated the government's resignation. Ramsay MacDonald remained as Prime Minister, however, at the head of a National government which included Baldwin and the leader of the Liberal Party, Sir Herbert Samuel. In addition to MacDonald only three members of the Labour Cabinet remained in office; Philip Snowden as Chancellor of the Exchequer, Lord Sankey as Lord Chancellor and J. H. Thomas who gave up the role of Lord Privy Seal and went to Dominions. Andrew Thorpe has observed that, up to 1931, the Labour Party was dominated by Ramsay MacDonald, Philip Snowden, Arthur Henderson, J. H. Thomas and J. R. Clynes.[17] The 1931 crisis removed MacDonald, Snowden and Thomas from the party and, as the 1930s drew on, both Henderson and Clynes became too old to provide leadership (indeed, the former died in 1935). Although George Lansbury became leader of the Labour Party, more significant was the emergence of a new generation of leaders which became the dominant group in the party up to 1945 and beyond. These were Clement Attlee, Ernest Bevin, Herbert Morrison, Sir Stafford Cripps and Hugh Dalton. Thus, although the immediate aftermath of the 1931 debacle was bleak for the Labour Party (it won only forty-six seats in the general election of that year) it enabled necessary rebuilding and policy formulation to take place. In particular, as Pelling has observed, 'the General Council of the TUC under the leadership of Bevin and Citrine abandoned its usual role of being sheet-anchor of the party and instead moved in to take the helm'.[18] At the 1935 general election the Labour Party made a substantial recovery, winning 154 seats and subsequently electing Clement Attlee as leader. In 1940 war with Germany once again brought the Labour Party into government when Attlee agreed to serve under Churchill in a coalition government.

The Ministry of Labour and National Service

The experiment of having a Minister of Labour and Permanent Secretary both drawn from the labour movement ended in November 1918 when Sir Robert Horne succeeded George Roberts. It was never repeated. Sir David Shackleton was forced to share the role of Permanent Secretary with a career civil servant, Sir James Masterson–Smith. When Masterson–Smith departed in 1921 he was replaced by H. J. (later Sir Horace) Wilson and Shackleton was moved sideways into the post of Chief Labour Adviser, finally retiring in 1925. Between 1918 and 1940 there were eleven Ministers of Labour whereas there were only four Permanent Secretaries, the last of whom remained in post until 1944. In this situation it was civil servants (most prominently Wilson in the 1920s and the Permanent Under Secretary, Sir Frederick Leggett, in the 1930s) who dominated the Ministry, extending their influence and expertise throughout the inter-war period.[19] The Ministry's policy, however, remained substantially the same as that developed by the Labour Department of the Board of Trade before the First World War. As Sir Godfrey Ince (Permanent Secretary at the Ministry from 1944 to 1956) put it, the aim was 'to encourage industries to set up their own voluntary negotiating arrangements and to settle their own disputes'.[20]

Between the wars the Ministry became active in the sphere of industrial training. In 1919 it took over responsibility for government sponsored training from the Ministry of Munitions which had pioneered the rapid training of unskilled men and women for work in the munitions industry. A separate department of the Ministry of Labour was established to administer schemes of training for disabled ex-service personnel and those who had enlisted in the armed forces before entering skilled employment, and whose prospects of gaining work were therefore limited. In the event, the onset of recession in 1920 served to confine the Ministry's early training schemes almost exclusively to the disabled. Of 88,000 men who received training between August 1919 and December 1924 only 6,000 were able-bodied.[21] Prolonged economic stagnation and the emergence of widespread unemployment served to bring about a rapid change in the nature of government sponsored training. Thus between 1925 and 1938 a range of schemes were initiated which, instead of providing high level skills for ex-servicemen, addressed the problems of re-training and rehabilitating the long term unemployed. During these years almost 2 million people received some form of training under the auspices of the Ministry of Labour. The vast majority of these (some 1.5 million) were young people under the age of 18 who had passed through junior instructional centres. Economic recovery in the later 1930s reduced the demand for government sponsored training and the Ministry of Labour's schemes began to be run down. With the outbreak of the Second World War, however, the Ministry (now of both Labour and National Service – MLNS) changed its priorities once again and expanded its activities to cope with the growing demand for semi-skilled munitions workers. Whereas in 1939 only sixteen government training centres were in existence, by 1940 the number had increased to thirty-five and, at the height of training activity in 1941, the number peaked at thirty-eight. In total more than 525,000 workers attended government training courses administered by the MLNS between August 1939 and July 1945.

Wartime expansion of the MLNS's role in industrial training was replicated in industrial relations generally. Experience gained during the First World War prompted government to adopt a programme of manpower planning which included military conscription and direction of labour. In return for supporting the government the trade unions demanded controls over pro-fiteering, maintenance of working class living standards and the restoration of pre-war practices on the cessation of hostilities. Further, conscious of their treatment after the First World War, they sought means of maintaining their influence in the post-war period. Meanwhile, the Labour Party penetrated far deeper into government than they had done during the period 1915 to 1918 and exercised much greater influence on the determination of policy. In all of these areas the central figure was Ernest Bevin who brought to the MLNS his vast experience as a trade union leader, organizer, negotiator and prominent figure on the General Council of the TUC. As Barnes and Reid have observed, Bevin

was, in effect, the trade union representative in the Cabinet and the key figure from the labour movement in the government. His major responsibilities were to achieve the highest level of war production and for this purpose to determine the allocation of labour between activities essential to the war effort, to contain the inflationary wage pressures ... and to avoid industrial trouble, which would have an adverse effect on the level of production.[22]

In carrying out these tasks Bevin was able to utilise a range of powers taken under the Emergency Powers (Defence) Act 1940. Orders were made to prevent workers from leaving essential jobs, to stop employers taking on workers except through labour exchanges, to direct workers to certain spheres of employment and also to regulate aspects of working conditions. Bevin's aim was to maintain as far as possible the conventions of voluntary collective bargaining whilst developing a corporatist consultation process involving representatives of government, employers, the TUC and individual trade unions. The sanctions provided under the Emergency Powers (Defence) Act were therefore held in reserve for use only when voluntary agreement proved impossible. Order 1305 of July 1940 prohibited strikes and required industrial disputes to be submitted to independent, binding arbitration. Although strike activity persisted throughout the war it never occurred on the scale experienced during the First World War. The annual loss of working days amounted to under 2 million per annum during 1939 to 1945 compared with over 4 million per annum during 1914 to 1918. Although between 1940 and 1945 over 100 prosecutions were made under Order 1305, its main value was, as MacDonald has noted, 'its moral effect: its prohibition of stoppages and the sanction of compulsory arbitration, which stimulated the parties to a dispute to exert every effort to make their own settlements'.[23]

The same spirit of consensus which served to restrain strike activity also brought about increased collaboration between employers, trade unions and the government. At industry level this was made manifest in the rapid expansion of Whitley Councils and the substantial extension of trade boards protection. At national level it was seen in the establishment of the National Joint Advisory Council and the Joint Consultative Committee which were constituted from members of the British Employers Confederation and the TUC, meeting under the chairmanship of Bevin at the MLNS. These bodies were charged with the task of advising the government about matters on which employers and workers had a common interest and, as Sharp has observed, 'few decisions of a major industrial importance were taken by the government during war time without prior consultation with the Council or the Committee'.[24] By the end of the war the relationship between government and the trade union movement had been transformed from one of indifference mingled with hostility to one of established partnership. The trade union movement had fully recovered its confidence and numerical strength, with membership increasing from a little over 6 million in 1939 to reach almost 9 million in 1946. War-time labour shortage enabled the unions to increase workers' wages by over 50 per cent in real terms during the period of the war[25] and, as we have seen, the traditions of collective bargaining were retained albeit within a framework of statutory restraint. Partnership was further nurtured by the unprecedented success of the Labour Party in the general election of 1945 which meant that many of the leading personalities from both wings of the labour movement (i.e. political and industrial) continued to collaborate during the early years of peace. In contrast to the widespread industrial unrest which characterised the years immediately following the First World War, 'the period of the Attlee government down to mid-1948 was one of relative peace on the industrial front. . . . The intimate, organic relationship of the TUC with the government, with such figures as Bevin in the Cabinet, ensured a close harmony of outlook between unions and ministers'.[26] The MLNS under Bevin held a pivotal role in government during the war and, when he left the Ministry for the Foreign Office in July 1945, it retained its prominence under George Isaacs.

Notes

1. Mowat C. *Britain Between the Wars*, Cambridge 1968 edition.
2. *Labour and Socialism: A History of the British Labour Movement 1867–1974*, Brighton 1983.
3. Wigham E. *Strikes and the Government 1893–1981*, 1982.
4. Pelling H. *A History of British Trade Unionism*, Harmondsworth 1976 edition.
5. Stevenson J. *British Society 1914–45*, Harmondsworth 1984.
6. Middlemas K. *Politics and Industrial Society*, 1979.
7. Report of Proceedings of the 49th Annual Trades Union Congress held at Blackpool 3–8 September 1917.
8. Mowat, op. cit.
9. op. cit.
10. Symons J. *The General Strike*, 1987 edition.
11. Lovell J. 'The TUC Special Industrial Committee, January–April 1926' in Briggs A. and Saville J. (eds) *Essays in Labour History 1918–1939*, 1977.
12. op. cit.

13. Wigham op. cit.
14. 'The Depression Years' in Pimlott B. and Cook C. (eds) *Trade Unions in British Politics*, 1982.
15. Taylor A. J. P. *English History 1914–45*, Oxford 1965.
16. Wigham, op. cit.
17. *The Failure of Political Extremism in Inter-War Britain*, Exeter, 1989.
18. *A Short History of the Labour Party*, 1982 edition.
19. Lowe R. 'The Government and Industrial Relations 1919–39' in Wrigley C. (ed.) *A History of British Industrial Relations*, Volume 2 1914–39, Brighton 1987.
20. *The Ministry of Labour and National Service*, 1960.
21. Cmd. 2481 Ministry of Labour Report for the Years 1923 and 1924, 1925.
22. 'A New Relationship: Trade Unions in the Second World War' in Pimlott B. and Cook C. (eds) *Trade Unions in British Politics*, 1982.
23. *The State and the Trade Unions*, 1976 edition.
24. Sharp I. *Industrial Conciliation and Arbitration in Great Britain*, 1950.
25. Marwick A. *British Society Since 1945*, Harmondsworth 1982.
26. Morgan K. *Labour in Power 1945–51*, Oxford 1984.

Chapter 5

The Limits of Consensus

The years 1939 to 1945 witnessed a major shift in the power of labour vis-a-vis capital and of the state vis-a-vis the individual. The enhancement of the power of labour, together with the restored numerical strength of the trade unions[1], reinforced the labour movement's resolve to avoid the problems of post-war depression experienced after 1920. The electoral verdict of 1945 was an indictment of what the electorate construed as Conservative inaction in the face of the high unemployment levels of the inter-war period. The success of the Labour Party, the development of the nationalisation programme and the creation of the National Health Service laid the foundations for a post-war political consensus built, above all, on a policy of full employment. However, Britain's position in the post-war world was much reduced and her damaged economy only restored by a combination of gifts, loans and austerity. The possibility of carrying through a radical transformation of Britain's economic and social structure was rapidly dissipated in the post-war period. Instead, successive governments sought to maintain full employment through the application of Keynesian economic techniques. Increasingly, the planning imperatives of demand management struggled to come to terms with the voluntaristic principles of the British industrial relations tradition. Although controls and interventions continued during the immediate aftermath of war, Britain's traditional pattern of industrial relations soon reasserted itself. The Wages Councils Act 1945 repealed the Trade Boards Acts 1909 and 1918 and maintained a safety net under the most vulnerable groups of workers. The Trade Disputes and Trade Union Act 1946 repealed the Act of 1927, restoring the 'contracting out' system and boosting the Labour Party's finances. The MLNS, however, gradually retreated and, when the Conservatives returned to power in 1951, the new minister, Walter Monckton, eagerly adopted a non-interventionist stance which stressed the value of voluntarism.

Full employment enhanced the bargaining power of the trade unions both nationally, through the continuing and growing influence of the TUC, and at workshop level through the sustained power of the shop stewards' movement. As a result overmanning, resistance to change and demands for increased pay continued unabated. The ability of the unions to eat into private sector profits and pre-empt public sector expenditure was increasingly cited as a central factor in Britain's poor economic performance vis-a-vis her major competitors. Successive governments struggled with balance of trade problems, comparatively low levels of economic growth, difficulties with the value of the pound, a stagnating economy and rising levels of unemployment. The country's industries remained under-capitalised, productivity levels were poor, formerly captive markets in the Commonwealth were lost and increased competition was experienced from countries both within and outside the European Community. Whilst the penetration of foreign manufactures into the British market increased, Britain's share of the world's exports of manufactured goods declined by 50 per cent between 1960 and the mid-1970s.

Attempts to manage capitalism, or sustain a mixed economy, won few friends in the labour movement. Britain's trade unions were torn between the impulse (largely rhetorical) to destroy capitalism and the imperatives associated with the demands of day to day collective bargaining. The outcome of this tension was an uncomfortable compromise; obstructive rather than constructive and generating an attitude inimical both to technical change and management innovation. During the long period of Conservative Government up to 1964, Britain's poor economic performance was increasingly blamed on poor industrial relations, particularly unofficial strikes, and attempts at reform began to force their way into political prominence. Whereas government had already taken on the task of maintaining full employment, it now moved towards accepting political responsibility for the efficient working of employment relationships based firmly on traditions of voluntarism and unrestrained collective bargaining. Irrespective of political party, the response of successive governments from the late 1950s to the late 1970s became essentially the same. Firstly, attempts were made in a series of incomes policies to curb wage inflation. Secondly, efforts were made to reform industrial relations either by exhortation or legislation as a means of achieving greater discipline, certainty and control. These attempts at reform, or put more crudely, efforts to reconcile contradictory variables, were all doomed to failure and contributed to the defeat of the Labour Government 1964–70, the Conservative Government 1970–74 and the Labour Government 1974–79.

Incomes policy and productivity bargaining

By the 1960s there was a growing body of opinion claiming that full employment and extensive unionisation were linked to wage inflation and low productivity. Fear of recession and unemployment, which had formed the backdrop to industrial relations before the Second World War, had been substantially removed and policy makers sought alternative methods of achieving wage restraint. In 1958 A. W. Phillips published *The Relationship Between Unemployment and the Rate of Change of Money Wage Rates in the United Kingdom 1861–1957* which suggested that a stable relationship between the level of unemployment and the rate of change in the level of wages had existed since 1861. Briefly, Phillips' research, and subsequent work by R. G. Lipsey, pointed to the unsurprising conclusion that excess demand for labour would cause wages to be bid upwards. From this position it could be convincingly argued that 'higher employment could be achieved only at the expense of higher wage inflation'.[2]

Given that full employment was the central plank of the post-war political consensus, policy makers were tempted to improve the trade-off between inflation and unemployment by intervening directly in the labour market through the imposition of incomes policy. In political terms incomes policy required government to persuade the electorate that the benign effects of intervention (i.e. sustained employment, international competitiveness for British products and lower levels of inflation) would outweigh the immediate loss in money wages. Trade unions in particular were required to moderate their pay claims – negotiating not for what the labour market would bear but within parameters arbitrarily set by government. The obvious immediate difficulty with incomes policy was that whilst governments were centrally concerned with employment in the aggregate, individual unions and workers were most often interested in a single sector or plant. The possibility of under-rewarding labour remained a constant problem as did grievances springing from the disturbance of historic differentials and relativities. Further, the vulnerability of the British economy to external factors such as currency fluctuations and increases in the price of major imports (most notably oil) meant that wage inflation was only one factor in a general trend of rising prices which gathered pace from the late 1960s to the early 1980s. Wage claims became a response to rising prices and an attempt by the unions to defend living standards.

As will be seen, the desire to obtain trade union co-operation with incomes policy forced governments to enter into negotiations with the TUC. In particular the Labour Government 1974–79 gave the trade unions a significant voice in policy making and were prepared to enact legislation favourable to the unions and workers at large. Even so the TUC and the trade union leaderships were unable to impose income restraint on their members for prolonged periods of time. Incomes policy was readily depicted as a means of disadvantaging workers by substantially reducing their capacity to bargain collectively. Periods of pay restraint provided another situation where unofficial leaders and the rank and file felt alienated from the official trade union leaderships. In terms of government's involvement, the economic gains which accrued from incomes policy were massively outweighed by the political costs. Briefly, governments staked their credibility on the success of a particular incomes policy initiative only to be embarrassed when the policy fell apart. This was most dramatically the case with the demise of the Labour Government in 1979, which is examined in detail in a subsequent section.

In 1960 the Esso Petroleum Company and the unions at its Fawley Refinery entered into an agreement which gave workers increased pay in return for changes in working practices. Specifically the unions agreed to reduce manning levels, eliminate overtime and exercise greater interchangeability and flexibility of labour in the performance of tasks. Increases in productivity resulted from changes in restrictive work practices rather than the introduction of new equipment or improvements in personal effort. Increased payments were a means of buying out existing custom and practice in order to achieve greater efficiency of operation. The new arrangements at Fawley received substantial attention with the publication of Allan Flanders' *The Fawley Productivity Agreements* in 1964 and they stimulated a vogue for various forms of incentive schemes including work study based bonuses and wage and salary restructuring programmes. Marsh has claimed that 'productivity bargaining was the most dynamic concept in British industrial relations in the 1960s'.[3] In part its popularity sprang from the circumstances created by the incomes policy put in place by Harold Wilson's Labour Government in 1964. In the *Declaration of Intent on Productivity, Prices and Incomes*, signed at Lancaster House on 16 December, the government agreed to establish machinery to monitor the movement of prices and incomes whilst 'management and the unions undertook to try to remove obstacles standing in the way of greater efficiency, and to assist the workings of the new prices and incomes machinery'.[4] The National Board for Prices and Incomes was established in 1965 and, between 1966 and 1969, produced three reports on productivity 'emphasizing the need to relate agreements to specific changes in working practices and to relevant indices of performance, to provide effective controls and to guard against repercussions elsewhere, as well as protecting the consumer'.[5]

The Labour Government's incomes policy for 1965 advocated a pay norm of 3 to 3.5 per cent with exceptions for productivity, manpower distribution and the removal of anomalies. The annual rate of inflation for that year was a little under 5 per cent and the trade unions therefore turned their attention to productivity bargaining as a means of obtaining the shortfall. Similar circumstances prevailed in 1966 when the government's incomes policy was given statutory underpinning which provided for a six month freeze on prices and pay, followed by six months of severe restraint. The annual rate of inflation for 1966 was a little under 4 per cent and declined to 2.5 per cent in 1967 before beginning the steady climb which took the figure to a peak of almost 25 per cent in 1975. Between 1967 and 1970 almost 4,000 productivity agreements were reported to the Department of Employment and Productivity.[6] No doubt many of these agreements did provide for some productivity improvements. Nevertheless there was a growing concern in government that many of the deals were spurious and aimed merely at evading the restrictive influence of incomes policy. Thus, although incomes policy continued intermittently until 1979, the popularity of productivity bargaining declined as the 1970s wore on and was eventually supplanted by the management led attack on restrictive work practices which was stimulated by the growth in unemployment.

In place of strife?

It has been observed in earlier chapters that there are close ties between the trade unions and the Labour Party. Personal, institutional and financial links provide an organic relationship between the industrial and political wings of the labour movement capable of being depicted as constructive or sinister, depending upon one's point of view. Although, as Colin Crouch has observed, the Labour Government which came to power in 1964 could not take the trade unions for granted it could nevertheless claim with justification that it was better fitted to deal with them than its Conservative predecessors.[7] Of course the Labour Party, whether in or out of power, always risks accusations that it is 'soft on the trade unions' or even controlled by them. It is in order to refute such claims during periods when it is in office (and also to appear capable of governing in the national rather than a sectional interest) that the Party has entered into confrontation with the unions as often as the Conservatives. As has been indicated in the previous section, the use of incomes policy is at all times a high risk strategy which invests considerable political credibility in attempting to influence or control negotiations which have traditionally been beyond the scope of governments during peacetime. In the longer term[8] the use of such policy is likely to bring any government into conflict with the unions as sectional interests within the trade union movement become restive. Where the Labour Party is concerned the likely outcome is to estrange the government at Westminster from activists in the constituencies and rank and file delegates to the TUC. The Labour Governments of the 1960s and 1970s attempted to steer a course between defending policies they considered essential to the national economy and the grass roots' accusation that they were merely shoring-up capitalism at the expense of the workers. What held good for incomes policy was found to be even more the case with restrictive legislation. The trade union movement has always looked to Labour in government to make their (i.e. the unions) life easier by passing beneficial (or repealing hostile) legislation. Indeed, as has been noted, this was central to the trade unions' support for the initial establishment of the Labour Party: the unions have not continued to fund the Party year after year merely to see their powers reduced when it is elected to office. Given all this it is not surprising that Labour's single attempt to enact legislation restricting the activities of the unions ended in outright failure.

In 1963 the case of Rookes v. Barnard cast doubt on the scope of trade union immunities under the Trade Disputes Act 1906. Mr Rookes had worked for the British Overseas Airways Corporation (BOAC) and, as a non-unionist, refused to join the Draughtsmen's and Allied Technicians' Association. BOAC operated a closed shop and, when the union threatened to strike over the issue of Rookes' non-membership, they dismissed him. It was held by the House of Lords, where the case went on appeal, that the union was guilty of intimidation and Rookes therefore entitled to damages. Once again a chink had appeared in the unions' immunities under the law and the TUC responded by pressing the government for legislation to remedy the situation.

In return they offered to accept the appointment of a Royal Commission to examine all aspects of trade union law. Faced with growing disquiet among the electorate concerning the power of the trade unions, and aware that a sizeable minority among their own backbenchers desired reform of trade union law, the Conservative Government announced that a Royal Commission would indeed be appointed. They added, however, that it would not be established until after the forthcoming general election and accordingly placed the proposal in their election manifesto. Crouch has observed that, although 'the government did not survive the election, the promise of a Commission, with some slight modification, did'.[9] Labour came to power in October 1964 and, in February 1965, announced the appointment of the Royal Commission on Trade Unions and Employers' Associations under the chairmanship of Lord Donovan. As a quid pro quo for the trade union movement's agreement to participate in the work of the Commission the government brought forward a Bill to deal with the difficulties created by the Rookes v. Barnard case and this became the Trade Disputes Act 1965.

Barnes and Reid account for the Labour Government's decision to proceed with the Conservative's proposal for an inquiry as follows:

The appointment of a Royal Commission might take the issue of industrial relations and trade union power out of politics for two or three years, and certainly for the period until the next general election. There was, also, always a hope that a Commission might eventually put forward proposals which would improve industrial relations, satisfy public opinion and be acceptable to the trade unions.[10]

By the time the Donovan Commission reported in June 1968 the relationship between the government and the trade unions had deteriorated badly. General economic difficulties, particularly the prolonged foreign exchange crisis which resulted in the devaluation of the pound in November 1967, precipitated deflationary measures which swept away the bulk of Labour's progressive programme. A growing belief among the rank and file of the unions that the government was demanding unjustified sacrifices from the workers through the imposition of incomes policy began to be shared by trade union officers, the TUC and a number of Labour backbenchers. On the government's side, the level of industrial unrest, particularly the very high incidence of unofficial strikes, led to the view that attempts to deal with a difficult economic and political situation were being sabotaged by the unreasonable actions of some trade unionists. Certainly this view was taken by the Prime Minister, Harold Wilson, and his Employment Secretary, Barbara Castle. As early as May 1966 Wilson had characterised an unofficial strike by the National Union of Seamen, in pursuit of a pay increase which breached the government's incomes policy, as the work of Communist agitators. By 1968 he had become convinced that the bulk of current strike activity was being stimulated by unrepresentative, militant shop stewards who, if not actually Communists, were certainly extreme left-wingers more interested in wrecking the British economy than negotiating constructively on behalf of their fellow workers. In the face of the electorate's growing demands that the government should 'do something about the unions' Wilson, strongly prompted by Castle, became increasingly attracted to the idea of trade union reform and the use of legislative intervention to discipline industrial disputes.[11]

The Donovan Commission claimed to identify two systems of industrial relations operative in Britain, viz. the formal and the informal. According to the Report 'the formal system assumed . . . most if not all matters appropriate to collective bargaining could be covered in industry-wide agreements'. The informal system, on the other hand, assumed 'bargaining in the factory . . . to be of equal or greater importance'.[12] These two systems were said to be in conflict, with the informal advancing at the expense of the formal. Whether the notion of system as applied to British industrial relations was useful remains problematical. Conventions of industrial relations practice differed from industry to industry and the claim that the myriad transactions which occurred could be generalised in the manner suggested by Donovan is dubious. Use of the word 'factory' in the above quotation provides an indication of the significance given to manufacturing, and particularly engineering, in the Commission's deliberations. Certainly, as we have seen, there was a prevailing tradition within industrial relations which included legal abstention and emphasised voluntarism. Obviously, however, a tradition and a system are conceptually and actually very different things and Donovan's confusion of the two allowed a deeply conservative Report to appear progressive. The reason for the pressures on national collective bargaining sprang immediately from the conditions of full employment which had prevailed since 1945 and enhanced the position of shop stewards. As we have seen labour shortages during both the world wars had created a similar situation and shifted the frontier of control between managers and the managed to the advantage of labour. At the time when the Donovan Commission were carrying out their work the national agreement still maintained its primacy in the public sector although this position was to change rapidly from the late 1960s onwards.

The central problem confronted by the Commission was how to inject discipline into workplace negotiations and thereby reduce the constant turbulence resulting from the threat and use of strike activity which disrupted industry and the economy far beyond the immediate context of a dispute. In the tight labour markets of the mid-1960s the Commission were, of course, aware that it was not possible to restore the centrality of national negotiations or to inject discipline by enabling levels of unemployment to increase. Instead, in the words of Robert Taylor, it 'favoured the introduction of more order into the informal system through . . . better facilities and greater recognition for the stewards by both unions and management. In other words, Donovan wanted to use voluntarism as the means of remedying the defects.'[13] The emphasis on the benefits of voluntarism were an attempt to seal off an alternative means of injecting discipline into industrial relations through an increase in legal intervention. Nevertheless, Andrew Shonfield in a Note of Reservation to the Report advocated a substantial extension of the law. In Shonfield's view the abstention of the law had become less and less defensible as society grew increasingly complex and ever more integrated. His chosen remedy was to make collective agreements enforceable contracts. Obviously this proposal flew in the face of everything the trade union movement had campaigned for since the nineteenth century. It did, however, have a certain attraction for some politicians and also the public, who saw an extension of the law as the obvious means of curbing what many perceived to be irresponsible behaviour on the part of trade unionists.

The ill-fated attempt by Harold Wilson and Barbara Castle to restrain trade union power through a change in the law has been detailed by Peter Jenkins in *The Battle of Downing Street* and it is not therefore intended to give a blow-by-blow account here. Barnes and Reid have characterised the government's problem as being 'how to go further than the Donovan Report and give (itself) a more positive role without causing serious conflict with the trade unions'.[14] Castle's solution to this problem was outlined in a White Paper, *In Place of Strife: A Policy for Industrial Relations*, published in January 1969. It contained a number of proposals, such as compulsory recognition, calculated to appeal to the unions and render them sympathetic to the acceptance of less palatable items. These consisted of legislative measures giving the government powers to impose conciliation pauses in unofficial strikes, deal with inter-union disputes and require compulsory ballots where official strikes were considered likely to damage the national interest. In comparison with Shonfield's proposals or the Conservative Party's policy statement on the reform of industrial relations, *Fair Deal at Work* published in April 1968, Castle's measures were modest enough. Nevertheless they met with widespread opposition from the trade union movement led by the new General Secretary of the TUC, Victor Feather, and also from a sizeable number of Labour backbenchers – particularly those enjoying trade union sponsorship.

When the Chancellor of the Exchequer, Roy Jenkins, announced in his Budget speech that the government would introduce a short Bill dealing with the issues of inter-union disputes and conciliation pauses in unofficial strikes, he precipitated the most damaging split between a Labour Government and the trade union movement since 1931. Initially Wilson and Castle were adamant that the Bill would become law. However, in the face of opposition led by James Callaghan within the Cabinet and the threat of a major backbench revolt Wilson was finally forced to climb down. Following prolonged negotiations he accepted a face-saving formula from the TUC – the famous 'solemn and binding undertaking' whereby the

TUC itself offered to intervene to solve inter-union disputes and unoffical strikes. The political fallout for Wilson and the Labour Government was considerable. Certainly it undermined public confidence in the government and substantially reduced Wilson's personal standing in the country. The influence, or perhaps more accurately power, of the TUC had undoubtedly been enhanced and the confidence of the trade union movement at large substantially boosted. Nevertheless, government attempts to reform industrial relations law were not over and when the Conservatives under Edward Heath took power in 1970 they immediately introduced far more radical proposals than those attempted by Labour.

The Industrial Relations Act 1971

The Conservative Party's decision to legislate to make collective agreements enforceable at law marked the end of the avoidance of confrontation with the trade unions as pursued by both Churchill and Macmillan. The change of policy did not occur overnight but shifted gradually, partly as a result of initial overt trade union collaboration with the Labour Government of Harold Wilson and partly in response to economic and electoral considerations. As we have seen Wilson's attempt to restrain trade union power through legislation had soured the relationship between the Labour Party and the unions. The Conservatives came to believe that they could succeed where Labour had failed and gain widespread electoral popularity as a result. In 1958 the Inns of Court Conservative and Unionist Society published a pamphlet, *A Giant's Strength*, in which it was claimed that the immunities enjoyed by the unions placed them beyond the rule of law and that legislation should be passed to bring them within it. This was the view taken in the Conservative's policy document *Fair Deal at Work*, adopted by the Shadow Cabinet at the Selsdon Park Hotel, Croydon, in January 1970 and included in the manifesto for the 1970 election.

The hardening of the Conservatives' attitude to the trade unions was stimulated by the conviction that Britain's economic recovery was linked to the successful reform of industrial relations. The level of unemployment had been increasing since the mid-1960s and, by 1970, stood at 2.5 per cent. The rate of inflation had increased from 5.4 per cent in 1969 to 6.4 per cent in 1970 and reached 9.4 per cent in 1971, by which time the level of unemployment had grown to 3.4 per cent. These figures, modest enough by more recent standards, were a problem for governments of both political parties and threatened the economic underpinning of the post-war consensus. Prime Minister Heath and his Employment Secretary, Robert Carr, were of course aware that the entire labour movement and a significant section of the electorate would be deeply hostile to legislation removing the trade unions' legal immunities. Indeed, the early introduction of the Industrial Relations Bill did much to heal the damaged relationship between the unions and the Labour Party as the two wings united to oppose it. Notwithstanding the risks, however, Heath and Carr were confident that the political and economic benefits of their legislation would in the long term far outweigh the costs. They were soon to be proved wrong.

The Industrial Relations Act 1971 attempted to shift British industrial relations away from voluntarist principles towards a framework of law. It established a new labour court, viz. the National Industrial Relations Court, and introduced a list of civil wrongs (known as unfair industrial practices) calculated to reform the relationship between unions and their members and also to regulate collective bargaining. Under the Act unions were required to register with a Trade Union Registrar who had the power to scrutinize and regulate their rules. Unions refusing to register lost the benefit of tax exemption on their provident benefits and, among other penalties, surrendered immunity against claims for damages for breach of employment contracts. The Act substantially ended the closed shop, although special provisions were made for certain exceptions such as the actors' union Equity. It also introduced emergency ballots and cooling-off periods for certain categories of industrial action. Finally, written collective agreements were deemed to be legally binding unless it was specifically stated to the contrary. In her critique of the 1971 Act Gill Palmer has claimed that it was presented as one of the most ambitious attempts to reconstruct a major social institution and . . . was the main plank of the government's domestic social and economic policy. By 1974 the Act was discredited (and) Labour returned to office . . . with the repeal of the Act as one of its most popular election pledges.[15]

Broadly speaking the 1971 Act was met with outright hostility by the TUC and the trade union movement at large. The unions were in a confident mood following the defeat of *In Place of Strife* and this was boosted by the success of the miners in a national strike during 1972. The number of days lost through strikes rose from 13.5 million in 1971 to almost 24 million in 1972 and although the figure fell to 7 million in 1973 the government's claim that the new legislation would bring greater order to industrial relations was soon shown to be flawed. As part of their tactics for the 1972 strike the miners used mass picketing to prevent the movement of coal stocks. At one site, Saltley coke depot in Birmingham, 6,000 pickets were deployed to successfully prevent coal being delivered. Further, in the building strike of 1972 flying pickets were used, moving from site to site to obstruct would be strike breakers. In both cases a new mood of militancy was in evidence and confrontation and violence occurred as the police attempted to maintain order. In the London docks a dispute over containerisation led ultimately to five shop stewards (the so-called Pentonville five) being gaoled for contempt of court after refusing to end their picket of a depot owned by Midland Cold Storage. A wave of strikes soon closed the whole of the London docks together with those of Liverpool and Hull, and sympathetic stoppages occurred in transport, engineering and newspaper printing. Although the shop stewards' imprisonment was ended after less than one week when the House of Lords, on appeal, found the union (TGWU) rather than the stewards responsible, considerable damage was done to the government's credibility. Further, the TUC's campaign to make the Act unworkable, by ensuring that unions deregister, was given a boost as a result of the strong resentment generated by the imprisonment of trade unionists.

Turbulence in industrial relations was paralleled, and to an extent generated, by severe economic difficulties which forced the government to jettison its policy of non-intervention in industrial matters and also to seek a new rapport with the TUC. Although the government's declared policy had been to let 'lame duck' industries go to the wall, the threat to major companies such as Rolls Royce led to the abandonment of the policy. Similarly the government's intention to avoid the use of incomes policy was soon abandoned and the Counter Inflation Act 1972 re-established statutory incomes policy with a five month freeze on pay, prices, rents and dividends. In such a situation employers were unwilling to become unnecessarily entangled in the Industrial Relations Act's provisions and generally inserted clauses into collective agreements stating that they were not to be considered as legally binding. Collective bargaining was in any case complicated enough as negotiators struggled to comply with the requirements of the government's incomes policy. On coming to power in 1970 the Conservatives had abolished the National Board for Prices and Incomes but, under the Counter Inflation Act 1973, they established a Pay Board and a Price Commission and outlined precise codes for the regulation of incomes and prices. Stage Three of the government's counter inflation policy, which operated from November 1973 until the dismantling of the machinery in 1974, required negotiators to operate within a framework permitting increases of up to 7 per cent on the total wage bill, or £2.25 per worker per week, up to a maximum of £350 per annum. An extra 1 per cent was available to correct anomalies, such as the erosion of differentials, which had developed as a result of incomes policy. Stage Three also provided for threshold payments to be made available should the Retail Price Index increase by over 7 per cent. This provision soon became an extreme embarrassment to the government as prices continued to rise rapidly throughout 1973 and 1974. Sked and Cook have calculated that an extra £4.40 per week was paid to some 10 million workers as a result of threshold payments.[16]

The provisions of Stage Three soon brought the government into direct confrontation with the unions on the issue of pay, as increases failed to keep pace with inflation and workers began to see their living standards eroded. The Arab–Israeli war of October 1973 resulted in oil shortages and a price hike which quadrupled the cost of Britain's oil imports and seriously affected

the country's precarious balance of payments. For many years
Britain had been increasing its dependence on imported oil and
reducing its requirements for home produced coal, particularly
in the crucial electricity supply industry. The oil price increase
partially restored the demand for coal and massively enhanced
the bargaining power of the coal miners and the National Union
of Mineworkers (NUM). In November 1973 the miners decided
to implement a ban on overtime and weekend working as a
means of obtaining pay increases in excess of the Stage Three
guidelines. The government refused to make an offer outside
of Stage Three and a crisis soon developed in electricity supply
which resulted in electricity being available to industry on only
three specified days each week. Continued attempts to settle
the dispute foundered on the provisions of Stage Three and the
determination of the government to defend its income policy
to the bitter end. Intervention by the TUC in January 1974,
offering to consider the miners as a special case and not to use
any increase they might gain as a precedent for claims by other
groups of workers, was met with scepticism by the government
and failed to resolve the dispute. When the NUM decided to
pursue their pay claim with an all out strike scheduled to begin
on 9 February, Prime Minister Heath decided to call a general
election on the issue of 'who governs Britain'. In the run up to
the election the Conservatives attempted to depict the miners'
action as a direct attempt to undermine or even overthrow the
democratically elected government. In contrast the Labour Party
offered an alternative policy based on co-operation, rather than
confrontation, with the trade unions. The result of the election
was a heavy defeat for the Conservatives, who lost thirty-six
seats, and a narrow victory for Labour who returned to power
as a minority government, Harold Wilson once again becoming
Prime Minister.

The limits of consensus

Barnes and Reid have commented that 'from 1974 until 1978 at
least the relations between the trade unions and the governments

of Harold Wilson and James Callaghan were greatly influenced by the reaction of both union leaders and politicians to the events which took place between 1969 and 1972'.[17] In the face of the obvious failures of statutory incomes policy and legislative intervention, the Labour Party were able to depict their organic relationship with the trade union movement as the only viable policy alternative and it was on this policy that Wilson and Callaghan staked the party's political credibility. Not surprisingly, when the relationship collapsed in a spectacular outburst of strike activity during the winter of 1978–9 the political fallout was highly damaging for Labour. As has been seen the labour movement's opposition to the Industrial Relations Act 1971 did much to repair the damaged relationship between the trade unions and the Labour Party. The most prominent outcome of this was the Social Contract, an arrangement whereby the TUC agreed to collaborate with a voluntary incomes policy in return for the repeal of the 1971 Act and some modest economic benefits.

Gill Palmer has observed that 'from August 1975 until August 1978 the TUC . . . actively supported a government incomes policy designed to reduce the real level of earnings in the hope of reducing unemployment, avoiding accelerating inflation and keeping the Labour government in power'.[18] On their return to power Labour did not adopt a formal incomes policy immediately, although the TUC did issue guidelines to negotiators. In 1975–6 a Stage 1 policy was agreed which provided for increases of £6 per week across the board but no increases for what were then considered the better paid (i.e. those earning over £8,000 per year). The flat rate increase disturbed historic relativities and differentials and the lack of an increase for the better paid generated further problems. In 1976–7 under Stage 2 of the policy, a limit of 5 per cent was placed on increases in total earnings, with a cash minimum of £2.50 and a maximum of £4 per week. In September 1976 the TUC called for a return to free collective bargaining with effect from August 1977. As a result no Stage 3 guidelines were agreed although the government, in its White Paper *The Attack on Inflation after 31 July 1977*, urged negotiators to limit claims to 10 per cent. Failure to reach agreement on the Stage 3 guidelines effectively ended the Social Contract and, by 1978, the government found itself in increasing difficulties with industrial relations and the economy. Unemployment rose from a little over 4 per cent in 1975 to reach over 6 per cent in 1978 and, although inflation fell back from the staggering peak of over 24 per cent in 1975 to under 16 per cent in 1977 and around 8 per cent in 1978, there was considerable latent demand for pay increases. This was particularly the case in the public sector where incomes policy had badly depressed pay levels relative to earnings in the economy as a whole, and the unions were under considerable pressure from their members to restore the position.

Tensions within the trade union movement ended the TUC's ability to continue their support for the government's incomes policy and, when the government decided on a 5 per cent pay limit for 1978–9, were unable to contain widespread industrial unrest. All might have been well for Labour had James Callaghan, who had replaced Harold Wilson as Prime Minister in April 1976, called a general election in the autumn of 1978. Instead, he decided to postpone it until 1979 with dire consequences for his party. Amid a series of pay claims averaging four times the government's published limit, Labour 'inched forward into the winter wastes'.[19] The first major blow to the government's incomes policy came in the private sector where, following a nine week strike, Ford car workers obtained a 15 per cent increase. Unlike British Leyland and Chrysler at the time, Ford was both profitable and efficient and their unions could see no sense, or justice, in enabling the company to underpay the workforce. As the rank and file saw it, if a company could afford to pay it should be constrained to pay, and the intervention of government incomes policy was seen as being in the employers' rather than the workers' interests. Trade union activists preferred free collective bargaining and the risks of the market, to incomes policy and attempts at economic planning. The fact that free collective bargaining might damage the Labour Government and bring about the return of the Conservatives was seen as being neither here nor there when it came to calculating short term strategy.

The immediate response of the government to the Ford settlement was to attempt the implementation of legal sanctions calculated to punish companies which settled above the 5 per cent pay limit. In the case of Ford the sanctions would have placed an embargo on the government purchase of cars, vans and ambulances from the company, although the number of vehicles involved was small. The use of sanctions was thus largely symbolic and it is unlikely that the government would have removed financial support from the company to build an engine plant in South Wales as the money was already committed. In the event, as Donoughue has noted

the legal sanctions supporting pay policy were defeated on a motion in the Commons . . . it was very damaging to the government's authority to be defeated in parliament on a central policy issue. Things were clearly slipping. By Christmas 1978 the government had effectively lost control of pay in the private sector, and there were numerous strikes looming in the public sector. . . . The problem for the government was that 15 per cent represented a total defeat for its main (indeed its only major) current policy objective . . . the defeat on sanctions in the private sector meant that Labour's only continuing policy of constraint applied to the public sector alone.[20]

In an attempt to limit the damage, the government sought a means of avoiding or at least delaying the impact of a 15 per cent going rate disrupting the public sector. No longer able to control events in the private sector the government announced the establishment of a comparability commission charged with measuring appropriate pay and service conditions for public sector workers by making comparisons with the private sector. On the face of it this approach was bound to compromise the government's whole counter-inflation policy by ensuring that private sector pay increases (often involving relatively small numbers of workers) were carried across to the big battalions of the public sector. In the long term the comparability experiment generated wage inflation and served to undo much of what the Labour government had achieved during the years of wage restraint. In the short term, however, as Harold Wilson's and James Callaghan's policy adviser candidly admits, 'it provided the government with a public sector plank in our attempts to construct a comprehensive long term policy, while also offering a bribe which might take some of the heat out of the immediate crisis in public sector pay claims'.[21]

The government's concession of pay comparability came too late to head off the gathering industrial unrest which reached its peak in the early weeks of 1979 when the low paid, public sector workers severely disrupted the activities of local government and the National Health Service. On 22 January the unions served notice of the 'Winter of Discontent' when 1.5 million workers took part in a nationwide day of action (or inaction, depending on your point of view). As Whitehead comments 'it was the most severe disruption the public had yet experienced. Roads went ungritted, rubbish uncollected, and in one macabre twist the dead on Merseyside were left unburied'.[22] The unions' approach was aimed at maximising the misery inflicted on the public in order to exert leverage on the government. In the political context of 1979 the unions' actions soon destroyed the credibility of the Labour Government's claim that it enjoyed a special relationship with the unions. Nevertheless, as they had done in 1969 over the *In Place of Strife* legislation, the Labour Party and the TUC sought to paper over the cracks which had appeared in their relationship in order to present at least the illusion of harmony to the electorate. In February 1979 they published a joint statement (or 'concordat') which

concerned itself with every issue of importance arising from the problems of the economy, inflation, pay and industrial relations which had been in dispute or discussion between governments and the unions for the last twenty years or more. . . . Desks in Whitehall and Congress House had been ransacked for good advice and declarations of intent.[23]

In spite of these attempts to create an impression of unity, industrial unrest continued unabated and it became patently clear that Labour's attempt to govern with the acquiescence of the trade union movement had failed. Meanwhile, a resurgent Conservative Party under the leadership of Margaret Thatcher was well aware of the growing unpopularity of the trade unions with the electorate, and was campaigning on the promise of far reaching trade union reforms if elected. When the general election took place on 3 May 1979 the Conservatives obtained a larger swing of popular support than had occurred since Labour won power in 1945. Labour's defeat emphatically ended the post war political consensus as the incoming Conservative Government allowed the workforce to be exposed, for the first time since the 1930s, to the unmitigated depredations of unemployment.

Notes

1. Membership of trade unions grew from just under 8 million (i.e. 39 per cent of the labour force) in 1945 to reach a little under 13 million (i.e. 54 per cent of the labour force) in 1979.
2. Davies, R. 'Incomes and Anti-Inflation Policy' in Bain, G. (ed.) *Industrial Relations in Britain*, Oxford 1983.
3. Marsh, A. *Concise Encyclopedia of Industrial Relations*, Farnborough 1979.
4. Sked, A. and Cook, C. *Post-War Britain*, Harmondsworth 1984 edition.
5. Marsh op cit.
6. The MLNS reverted to the Ministry of Labour with the ending of National Service. In May 1968 the Ministry was renamed the Department of Employment and Productivity and placed under a Secretary of State. The words 'and Productivity' were removed by the Conservative Government which came to power in 1970.
7. *The Politics of Industrial Relations*, 1982.
8. 'Longer term' in this context means two or three years.
9. Ibid.
10. *Governments and Trade Unions: The British Experience 1964–79*, 1980.
11. Sked, A. and Cook, C. *Post-War Britain*, Harmondsworth 1984 edition.
12. Cmnd. 3623 Royal Commission on Trade Unions and Employers' Associations 1965–1968 para. 143.
13. 'The Trade Union Problem Since 1960' in Pimlott, B. and Cook, C. (eds) *Trade Unions in British Politics*, 1982.
14. Op cit.
15. *British Industrial Relations*, 1983.
16. Ibid.
17. Ibid.
18. Ibid.
19. Whitehead, P. *The Writing on the Wall* 1986 edition.
20. Prime Minister, 1987.

21. Donoughue op cit.
22. Ibid.
23. Ibid.

Chapter 6

The Alternative Policy

The Keynesian consensus which had dominated British economic policy since 1945 was under practical challenge throughout the 1970s. The phenomenon of 'stagflation', which saw low growth going hand in hand with escalating inflation, raised the spectre of hyper-inflation and the dire social consequences associated with monetary collapse. On the political left, Keynesianism was depicted as an ongoing programme of emergency measures calculated to postpone the final crisis of capitalism. On the political right, it was increasingly associated with weak government, national decline and the unhealthy prominence of the trade unions. Nevertheless, Keynesianism maintained its dominance of the political middle ground without a serious rival and it was only when the middle ground itself collapsed that a credible alternative economic paradigm finally emerged. Of course the new paradigm, i.e. monetarism, did not arrive out of nowhere but had been gathering support for many years. Resistance to its influence sprang, at least in part, from an inherent reserve among policy makers to sound money principles dating from the experience of the recession years of the 1920s and 1930s. It was the apparent inadequacies of Keynesianism itself which provided the opportunity for 'the capture of government by the monetarists'.[1]

In the context of the late 1970s monetarism's greatest attraction was its claim to offer a cure for inflation. Inflation had peaked at over 24 per cent in 1975 and, after declining to single figures in 1978, climbed to 18 per cent in 1980. It was of course known that applying monetarist inspired policies to reduce inflation would generate many painful side effects. Not least an increase in unemployment was likely to result, together with reductions in the level of public services and further decline in Britain's manufacturing base. All of this was likely to be electorally damaging and flirtations with monetarism by Roy Jenkins in 1968, Edward Heath in the early 1970s and Denis Healey in 1976 had all been abandoned in favour of a return to Keynesian orthodoxy. It was only when Keynesianism and consensus politics were able to be depicted as outright failures that the political risks associated with monetarism became worth the gamble. This moment came when Callaghan's accord with the trade unions finally collapsed, bringing the Conservatives to power with a leader fully committed to monetarist principles. As Smith has observed 'Margaret Thatcher was, more than anyone else, responsible for turning (monetarism) into a potent political idea . . . no other politician, even in countries with a much longer tradition of sound money . . . invested so much political capital in this particular economic philosophy'.[2]

The main lines of the Conservative's alternative strategy were put forward during 1977 in *The Right Approach to the Economy* which included much of what was eventually termed Thatcherism including monetarism, control of public expenditure and reform of the trade unions. Public expenditure control was to go hand in hand with a reduction in the activities of the state and a diminution in the significance of the public sector of the economy. The preferred method for reducing the scope of the public sector was privatisation and the incoming Thatcher government soon began to divest itself of financial winners and losers. This process was extended to the former heartlands of the public sector (i.e. the once apparently untouchable utilities of the post-war mixed economy) with the sale of British Gas, the water industry and the planned privatisation of electricity supply – albeit under conditions of tight regulation.[3] Additionally, a policy of contractualisation was adopted which eventually forced the local authorities and the National Health Service to place elements of their work out to competitive tender. These policies generated a number of outcomes. Firstly, there was a net gain to the Treasury from the proceeds of privatisation – the sale of British Airways and the British Airports Authority, for example, yielded in the region of £2,000 million.[4] Secondly, the government was largely able to resist political pressures to subsidise failing enterprises even though this had the side effect of allowing an accelerated reduction of the country's manufacturing base and a steep increase in the level of unemployment which rose steadily from a little over 5 per cent in 1979 to reach 13.5 per cent in 1985 before falling back to under 6 per cent in 1989.[5] The application of the 'market forces' approach substantially reduced the scale of operation, for example, of the indigenous motor industry with the Rover Group (formerly British Leyland) eventually becoming part of privatised British Aerospace. Thirdly, privatisation and contractualisation provided employers with the opportunity to attack historic work practices, introduce new technology and reassert management control. All of these changes had adverse effects on the trade union movement, particularly those unions such as the National Union of Mineworkers who saw their membership more than halved between 1980 and 1987. Finally, the government increasingly disassociated itself from the flux of industrial society, thereby resisting trade union attempts to argue over the heads of management and largely insulating itself from the political costs of industrial unrest. As will be seen, even during the bitter miners' strike of 1984–5 the government succeeded in keeping the issue at arms length, refusing to be panicked into direct intervention.

The Conservative Government's arms length approach to industrial relations was assisted by its refusal to use the device of a formal incomes policy. Whereas, as we have noted, governments during the previous twenty years or so up to 1979 had invested much of their political credibility in the attempt to control pay movements, the governments of Margaret Thatcher placed their faith in market forces and an apparent belief in the natural rate of unemployment. Confidence in the utility of the market also stimulated government inspired attempts to increase labour market flexibility by limiting the protection previously enjoyed by wage earners. Privatisation and contractualisation were accompanied by the rescinding of the Fair Wages Resolution, the initial reduction and later neglect of the wages councils and a series of statutes calculated to constrain the activities of the trade unions by substantially reducing their legal immunities. Further, the government placed pressure on employers to abandon national collective bargaining and adopt local negotiations as a means to exploit opportunities provided by different labour markets in various parts of the country. The crucial backdrop to all of this was, of course, the historically very high level of unemployment which we have noted and which tended to stimulate a general feeling of insecurity among working people.

The high unemployment/market forces strategy adopted by Margaret Thatcher carried with it substantial political risks which did not go unnoticed by the 'wetter' members of her party or, indeed, Cabinet. The Conservatives' aversion to high unemployment stemmed, as we have seen, in part from an interpretation of their defeat at the hands of Labour in 1945 when the Conservatives had been depicted as the party of unemployment, having largely presided over the inter-war years of recession. Unlike the Heath government, the Conservatives after 1979 did not rush to place comprehensive industrial relations legislation on the statute book on the model of the Industrial Relations Act 1971. Instead, they initially adopted a placatory approach with the moderate James Prior becoming Secretary of State for Employment and piloting the modest Employment Act 1980 through parliament. Not surprisingly, as unemployment rose rapidly during the early 1980s, and Prior gave way to the more abrasive Norman Tebbit, the opposition parties and the TUC clung to the belief that the Conservatives would inevitably be swept away on a tide of popular protest to electoral disaster. When this did not occur, and Margaret Thatcher emerged victorious at the general elections of 1983 and 1987, it became apparent that the political costs were not in fact accruing to the Conservatives but to the opposition parties and the TUC. For much of the 1980s the Labour Party manifested greater internal division than at any time since the Second World War and it was only at the very end of the decade that it began, under the leadership of Neil Kinnock, to once again appear to be a viable party of government.

The decline of the unions

It may be plausibly argued that trade union power grew steadily throughout the post-war period. Total membership rose from under 9.4 million in 1948 to peak at almost 13.3 million in 1979 and the influence of the TUC was in part increased by this sustained growth. The TUC's influence was also enhanced by economic policy, including modest attempts at corporatist planning, which brought it into regular consultation with government. The use of incomes policy was another means by which the trade union movement gained in influence as governments sought to control wage inflation by curbing collective bargaining. As we have seen attempts by governments to legislate against the unions during the late 1960s and early 1970s failed miserably. The Labour Government after 1974 sought to 'buy off' the unions with a combination of beneficial legislation and the offer of a bigger say in policy formulation. The exact extent of this 'say', like the notion of trade union power itself, is contentious and Taylor, for example, has claimed that although 'union leaders won greater access to Downing Street and government departments during the 1974–79 period . . . in no sense were they dictating to the Government and while their advice and demands were invariably listened to they were seldom acted upon'.[6] Nevertheless although there were obvious limits to the trade union movement's capacity to influence policy both nationally and at plant level, they at least possessed the negative ability to obstruct change and cause massive economic damage. Linked to this was the public perception, nurtured in the media and demonstrated in opinion polls, that the unions had too much power. The events of the 'Winter of Discontent' added further to the trade unions' growing unpopularity with the electorate and this meant that in any subsequent major confrontation between the unions and government, public sympathy was likely to be with the latter.

The incoming government of Margaret Thatcher had no intention of encouraging the trade union movement. The 'Winter of Discontent' had conclusively demonstrated the futility of pursuing trade union compliance through a corporatist strategy. The apparatus of corporatism was gradually dismantled and the influence of the TUC steadily eroded as government abandoned consultation. Under the impact of unemployment trade union membership declined by 2.6 million between 1979 and 1985 with the result that some unions were forced to surrender their independence through merger or takeover. In the public sector (where unions such as NALGO and NUPE had enjoyed rapid growth during the years of rising public expenditure) cuts in government spending reversed the trend. In the steel industry the first of a number of bitter defensive strikes was fought during 1980. It lasted 13 weeks and was followed by the implementation of new working agreements which led to the number of workers employed in the industry being reduced from 166,000 to 70,000 during the next three years.[7] Membership of the ISTC, the main union in the industry, fell from over 100,000 in 1980 to 68,000 in 1987. The job losses were not, however, without point as the steel industry was returned to profitability and the private sector. Government and employers sensed new possibilities for change and the era of 'macho management' was born. The steel dispute formed the backdrop to the passing of the Employment Act 1980, the first of the Thatcher Governments' legislative measures calculated to reduce trade union immunities. The Act restricted sympathetic and secondary industrial action by the unions and was followed by a further Employment Act in 1982. In the words of Palmer, the effect of these statutes was to 'exclude from legality vast areas of industrial action which had been seen as lawful for over six decades'.[8] The scenes of industrial militancy depicted on television during the steel dispute were useful to the government in justifying the need for legislation. As Hartley, Kelly and Nicholson have observed 'the steel strike . . . was a useful background against which the government could gain legitimacy for its legal measures. In many ways the government . . . were the winners of the strike'.[9]

As unemployment grew and Britain's manufacturing base suffered further decline under the impact of recession, the trade union movement placed its faith in the early return of a Labour Government. This possibility was, however, diminished by the damaging split between the right and left of the Labour

Party which culminated in the creation of the Social Democratic Party. In the general election of 1983 a weakened Labour Party, under the unlikely leadership of Michael Foot, polled only marginally more votes than the Social Democrats in alliance with the Liberals. The Conservatives increased their parliamentary majority from 43 to 144 seats, giving them the largest majority since 1945. With a new mandate the Conservatives pushed forward with the next phase of their industrial relations legislation which gained statutory form in the shape of the Trade Union Act 1984. The Act required that, in order to qualify for immunity, official strikes should be preceded by a ballot of all the union members involved. This was already the practice in unions such as NALGO and seemed not unreasonable to the public at large. The trade union movement, however, was placed in a quandary. With its hopes of a change of government shattered, it was faced with the alternatives of compliance or confrontation which placed tremendous pressure on trade union unity.

Within the trade union movement there were strongly varying views as to the appropriate response to what the bulk of the unions perceived as a continuous attack on their immunities. At the TUC the general secretary, Len Murray, urged a cautious, pragmatic approach characterised as the 'new realism'. This was echoed by the leaderships of the AEU and the traditionally moderate GMB. By contrast the response of the EETPU, led by Eric Hammond, was to take a radical approach to the new situation, even welcoming the new legislation and being prepared to enter into single union agreements and no strike deals. Hammond's policy, followed to a lesser extent by Terry Duffy, Gavin Laird and later Bill Jordan at the AEU, was calculated to break out of the bygone conventions of the labour movement, abandoning the mythology of class struggle and advocating a form of business unionism on the American model. Hammond's policy, which included recruiting in areas of industry traditionally covered by other unions, ultimately led to his union being expelled from the TUC. In contrast to Hammond, and those moderates advocating the 'new realism', there also existed within the trade union movement a number of traditional die-hards, perhaps most prominently represented by Arthur Scargill of the NUM. Scargill's approach, based on a quasi-Marxist analysis of society and containing a streak of syndicalist direct action, was very much at odds with the cautious attitude of Murray at the TUC and the business unionism pioneered by Hammond. Whereas Hammond's policy was calculated to exploit the possibilities presented by new technology and industrial change to the advantage of his union and its members, Scargill aimed to use a defensive strike in a declining industry to pursue a far wider purpose. Briefly, he sought to use industrial unrest to destabilise the government.

The Miners' Strike 1984–5

The coalminers have always occupied a special position in the labour movement. The harshness of the work, the solidarity of mining communities and the significance of coal in the development of the British economy have all combined to form a potent myth. For many Labour activists and socialist intellectuals the hazardous life of the coalminer still engenders a sense of guilt and unworthiness. Compared to coalmining most working lives are soft and miners' leaders have never been reluctant to remind anyone prepared to listen of this fact. As we have noted the miners played the leading role in the General Strike of 1926 and also the industrial unrest which destabilised the Heath Government during the early 1970s. In spite of coalmining's prominence in the sphere of labour relations, however, the industry has been in long term decline throughout the bulk of the present century. In 1914, as Pagnamenta and Overy have observed,

there were over a million coalminers in Britain (and) the number was still rising, because coal dominated the economy. Coal had allowed the country's massive industrial advance to occur and had determined the areas of Victorian Britain in which it took place. The coal was brought up from 3,000 pits and fuelled not only steel, engineering and textiles but provided the raw material for the new electrical and chemical concerns. Coal was needed for the railways and the gasworks, and was one of Britain's greatest exports.[10]

Britain largest ever output of coal was achieved as long ago as 1913 when 278 million tons were extracted. As we have seen the inter-war history of the industry was deeply troubled and it was not until nationalisation occurred in 1947 that the necessary investment was forthcoming to bring about rationalisation and modernisation. In spite of the fact that many of the pits were not economically viable, it was assumed that demand for coal would go on increasing and that all coal production, however costly, was worth having. In reality the reverse was the case as technological change, together with competition from deep mined and open cast coal from abroad, steadily eroded demand. In 1957 the National Coal Board (NCB) produced 223 million tons of coal, in 1961 the figure was 190 million tons and in 1966 it was 173 million tons. Between 1957 and 1970 the number of pits fell from well over 800 to under 300 and the number of miners employed in the industry from 700,000 to under 300,000. In almost every sphere where coal had been the dominant fuel demand fell steeply. Domestic use declined under the impact of Clean Air legislation; in shipping and railways coal was no longer required; in the gas industry coal gave way to natural gas. Only in electricity supply did coal maintain its prominence and even there it came under increasing competition from cheap oil and nuclear energy.

The coal industry gained a reprieve from seemingly inexorable decline by the hike in oil prices which followed the Arab–Israeli war of October 1973. Oil prices quadrupled and, as has been noted in an earlier chapter, partially restored the demand for coal and massively enhanced the bargaining power of the coalminers and the National Union of Mineworkers (NUM). When Labour came to power in 1974 it produced a *Plan for Coal* which aimed to increase coal production from the current figure of 130 million tons per annum to almost 140 million tons by 1985. As Adeney and Lloyd have noted the effect of this change on the NCB was that 'thinking had to be stood on its head. From managing gradual decline engines had to be reversed once again and the vast enterprise pointed towards expansion'.[11] Managing this change fell to the NCB chairman, Sir Derek Ezra and the president of the NUM, Joe Gormley – both ultimately destined to enter the

House of Lords as life peers. Raised production targets were being achieved during the late 1970s but, as so often in the past, the coal industry once again fell victim to the vagaries of the market. In 1982–3 the NCB recorded a deficit of £485 million and the need to adjust to reduced demand stimulated NCB plans to bring about the accelerated closure of so called 'uneconomic' pits. The shift in market conditions coincided with a shift in attitudes within the NUM (as Arthur Scargill replaced Joe Gormley), and within government as Margaret Thatcher felt greater security in office following the Conservative's election victory in 1983. Whereas Ezra and Gormley had managed to operate on the basis of bipartisan collaboration there was to be no such relationship between Arthur Scargill and Ezra's successor, Ian MacGregor. It was the shift in attitudes together with adverse economic circumstances which precipitated the 1984–5 miners' strike.

In their book *The Miners' Strike 1984–5: Loss Without Limit*, Martin Adeney and John Lloyd provide a detailed account of the bitterest industrial dispute to occur in Britain since 1926. It is not intended to replicate their work in the present text; instead a number of salient points will be made. Arthur Scargill's determination to press forward with strike action without holding a national ballot placed tremendous strain on the unity of the NUM. Ultimately the failure of the striking miners to persuade (or coerce) their working colleagues to join the strike resulted in the creation of a breakaway union, the Union of Democratic Miners, based largely in Nottinghamshire. The lack of solidarity among the miners, together with legal sanctions against secondary action, determined that other trade unions were reluctant to provide support beyond making financial contributions to the NUM's strike fund. The steelworkers, for example, were unwilling to risk their jobs in support of the miners. In the case of the key unions in the electricity supply industry (i.e. the EPEA and the EETPU) their leaderships were deeply out of sympathy with Scargill and his methods. The value of flying pickets and mass picketing was limited by tough policing and MacGregor's determined management. Although there was substantial public sympathy for the miners' case, there was also a general feeling that defeat of the NCB, and by extension the government, would result in political disaster. The TUC's attempts to mediate in the dispute met with failure and the Labour Party were embarrassed as they sought to distance themselves from the ever growing violence on the picket lines while appearing sympathetic to the miners' case. In the event the miners returned to work without a negotiated settlement. Although Scargill claimed a victory this hardly seems justified by objective examination of the evidence. The NUM ended the dispute divided and with its finances in chaos. The pace of pit closures accelerated rapidly in the aftermath of the dispute and the number of miners employed by the NCB declined dramatically. As Lloyd and Adeney observe:

By the time the NUM and the UDM held their conferences in mid-summer 1986, twenty-seven pits had been shut since the strike, with another five closures agreed and two more proposed. The number of people employed by the NCB had shrunk from over 234,000 when the strike had begun to little more than 175,000. At collieries the decline was steeper, from 181,000 to 133,000 – more than a quarter.[12]

The decline of the coal industry continues and, at the time of writing, there is speculation in the press of further deep cuts in the labour force as British Coal (as the NCB is now known) struggles to maintain its market share in the face of foreign competition, and growing concern over the environment and the adverse effects of burning coal for the generation of electricity. In terms of industrial relations considerations the failure of Scargill and the miners to defeat the NCB, let alone bring down Margaret Thatcher and the government, had a substantial impact. As Riddell has observed,

with the eventual defeat of the strike Mr Scargill's confrontational approach, vanguardism, was discredited, both within his own union and more generally. The result had both practical and symbolic importance in dramatically underlining the shift of trade union power. Other union leaders, and their members, took note and the end of the dispute was followed by the lowest level of strike activity for fifty years.[13]

The search for labour market flexibility

The Thatcher Governments have manifested tremendous faith in the utility of markets. In the sphere of industrial relations the bulk of their effort has been calculated to free up the labour market, increase competition and improve productivity. The slow accretion of custom and practice at the workplace; the safety net provided by full employment policy; the strength of the trade unions; the comfort provided by the welfare state and council housing, were all viewed as barriers to essential change. Margaret Thatcher's animosity to the dependency culture was intimately linked to her desire to restore Britain's economic position. As we have seen, the abandonment of full employment policy, together with the retreat of the state from many areas of industry, was calculated to confront workers and unions with a clear choice between moderating their pay claims or facing redundancy. Seen in this light the long series of legislative measures aimed at reducing trade union immunities, can be seen as attempts to improve labour market flexibility by diminishing workers' capacity to resist change. Privatisation and contractualisation can also be interpreted as devices calculated to stimulate change and encourage managers to implement new work practices and introduce new technologies. The Thatcher Governments have held doggedly to the view that the private sector, with its emphasis on the profit motive, is inherently more efficient than the public sector with its emphasis on service. The fact that the vast majority of the population's perception of public sector organizations (with the possible exception of the National Health Service) was one of endemic inefficiency and waste, guaranteed widespread popular support for the government's policies. Where privatisation was not a viable possibility, the imposition of cash limits and an increase in external scrutiny through audit acted as a surrogate for the profit motive.

Parallel with government inspired attempts to stimulate flexibility of labour utilisation were efforts to introduce greater flexibility into the arrangements for determining pay. Again the government placed great emphasis on the benefit of the unfettered market mechanism; rescinding the Fair Wages Resolution, attacking and quietly neglecting the wages councils, abolishing the National Dock Labour Scheme and advocating an end to national collective agreements. Although the government were prepared to maintain review bodies for certain groups of workers which they considered to be essential (e.g. police, fire fighters and nurses) it generally set its face against the use of comparability studies for the determination of pay, abolishing the Civil Service Pay Research Unit in 1980 and firmly resisting the ambulance workers' demand for a review body in 1989–90. Government's dislike of national collective agreements sprang from two main sources. Firstly, the belief that the annual pay round, resulting in a nationally promulgated figure, was unnecessarily costly and insufficiently linked to improvements in productivity. Instead the government preferred pay negotiations to take place at individual or plant level where greater emphasis could be placed on performance. Briefly, reward linked to achievement rather than the 'going rate'. Secondly, government took the view that national agreements tended to displace rates of pay necessary to recruit and retain staff in London and the South East to other areas of the country where they were excessive.

The Thatcher Governments' attempts to stimulate labour market flexibility certainly met with considerable success. Evidence of impressive productivity improvements in steel, coal mining, motor manufacturing, newspaper printing, local government and elsewhere suggest that many of the barriers to change have been overcome, albeit at the cost of large numbers of jobs. Greater economic activity, particularly in the service sector of the economy, also created many jobs although these may prove to be perishable. In the case of pay levels the situation was less than satisfactory. In spite of historically high, though gradually diminishing levels of unemployment, throughout the 1980s average earnings in Britain rose at a much faster rate than those of her major industrial competitors. At the time of writing, in mid-1990, inflation is on a rising trend, pay settlements are nudging 10 per cent and unemployment is showing a modest increase. Already a certain nervousness can be detected in government concerning the risks of leap-frogging as employers outbid each other in pursuit of scarce skilled labour. It appears that high numbers of unemployed may have less influence on restraining pay demands than has sometimes been thought. Although, as has been seen, the trade unions have been weakened, institutionalised collective bargaining remains a central factor in British industrial relations and will continue to do so for the foreseeable future. We will return to consider the extent to which Margaret Thatcher's alternative policy has really changed things in the next chapter. The remainder of the present chapter will be devoted to a case study (i.e. the water supply industry) where privatisation and an end to national collective bargaining have developed in tandem.

Case study: the water supply industry

The passing of the Water Act 1973 brought about a radical restructuring of the water industry in England and Wales. The Act consolidated responsibility for the management of all aspects of water usage into the hands of ten new regional water authorities (RWAs). In place of a fragmented industry with strong local government connections, the RWAs provided a high level of organizational integration on a quasi-nationalised basis.[14] Local authorities maintained a residual interest in the industry through membership of the boards of the new regional bodies. Local authority members served on the boards together with members directly appointed by the Secretary of State for the Environment and the Minister of Agriculture. Membership of each board was thus of a hybrid nature expressing a tension between the desire for a modicum of local accountability and the requirements of technological expertise and efficiency. This tension was subsequently resolved by the provisions contained in the Water Act 1983 which terminated local authority membership and replaced the large, hybrid boards with small memberships entirely appointed by the Secretary of State for the Environment. Local authority representation was limited to membership of new consumer consultative committees.

The 1973 Act posed major problems in terms of integrating the numerous bodies responsible for various aspects of the water industry into the RWAs. To assist in this process, and to provide a consultative forum with central government, a new statutory body – the National Water Council (NWC) was established. The NWC brought together the government (in the form of the Department of the Environment), the RWAs and the private water companies represented by the Water Companies Association (WCA). The 1983 Act abolished the NWC and a new voluntary central forum for the industry was created called the Water Authorities Association (WAA) – now the Water Services Association – consisting of representatives of the RWAs and the WCA. In February 1985 the government announced its intention to privatise the water industry. Among the water authorities Thames, the largest of the RWAs and successor body to the Metropolitan Water Board, was the most enthusiastic for privatisation and its chairman Roy Watts suggested a timetable for privatisation of the industry by the summer of 1987. In the event, opposition from within and outside the industry precluded privatisation under the Conservative administration of 1983–87. When, however, the Conservatives were returned in June 1987 progress towards privatisation was rapid. As a means of overcoming objections concerning water quality the government, under the Water Act 1989, established the National Rivers Authority (NRA) hived off from the activities of the RWAs.

Regionalisation of the water industry into ten autonomous authorities (plus the existing water companies) rapidly shifted the employers' perceptions of collective bargaining requirements. The sheer size of the regions tended to increase the attraction of local autonomy rather than reinforce dependence on district or national level negotiations. These latent tendencies were accelerated by changes brought about under the 1983 Act. Whereas the Water Act 1973 had imposed a statutory industrial relations system on the industry, the 1983 Act restored a voluntary system. Further, the demise of the NWC demonstrated government's acceptance that the task of rationalising the industry was complete. When a national strike occurred in the industry during 1983 it served to increase the employers' reserve about the benefits of national negotiations. However, the employers' threatened abandonment of national bargaining provoked the threat from the trade unions that they would maintain their national negotiating teams and pick off the RWAs one by one, thereby generating a process of leap-frogging. In the context of 1983 (i.e. prior to the passage of the Trade Union Act 1984 and the defeat of the miners), the government and the employers were not entirely confident of being able to face down the unions in perhaps the most crucial of industries. A confidential report was therefore commissioned (i.e. the Ramsay report) and, following its recommendations, a compromise was struck.

In September 1983 new negotiating bodies were established for the water industry and national negotiations were continued. Within the WAA the Water Industry Central Manpower Unit was created and headed up by a chief negotiator recruited not, as traditionally, from the water industry or local government but from the Ford Motor Company. There was thus a marked change in negotiating style with the unions placed on the defensive during a period of historically high unemployment, manpower reductions, hostile legislation and the constant threat of losing national negotiations and agreements. Further, the new national agreements which were drawn up stripped out much of the detailed material from the former agreements, which had accrued over the previous sixty-five years, and delegated the bulk of day-to-day industrial relations matters to local level. No district structure was adopted and national negotiations were limited to relatively few central, substantive areas such as rates of pay, hours of work, overtime rates, holidays, sick pay, stand-by and call out payments.

Certainly, in terms of the employers' objectives, the new national agreements appear to have worked well. No major industrial unrest occurred, substantial manpower reductions were achieved through natural wastage, productivity increased and the annual manual worker wage bill was reduced by 2.4 per cent (i.e. £5 million per annum) between 1984 and 1988. Nevertheless, scepticism concerning the benefits of national bargaining arrangements persisted among the employers; most prominently Thames which, at the end of 1986, served notice of its intention to quit the NJIC in December 1987. The WAA commissioned a further report on collective bargaining arrangements in the industry which recommended the maintenance of the existing system. In spite of this, however, Thames were determined to go it alone and were eventually joined by

Northumbrian. The government's announcement of its plans to privatise the water industry struck the final death knell for national negotiations. The possibility of maintaining a residual, central organization in London to act in an advisory capacity, collecting and monitoring statistical information on industrial relations, was abandoned. The Water Industry Central Manpower Unit was finally closed down in October 1989, ending central negotiations in the industry after a period of seventy years.

Several factors influenced the ending of national negotiations in the water industry. Certainly regionalisation created very large operating units which tended to stimulate the demand for local autonomy. Further, as the RWAs matured and the calibre and expertise of their personnel officers improved there was a growing desire to be 'masters in their own house' rather than delegating negotiations to an external body. The trend, under the government's prompting, towards local bargaining as opposed to national negotiation was also influential. Finally, the crucial issue of privatisation appeared to offer unique opportunities to change working practices and patterns of reward. The notion that national negotiations were tending to displace rates of pay necessary to recruit and retain staff in London and the South East to areas of the country where lower rates would be more appropriate, was a consideration at only a rhetorical level. Thames were by far the highest payers and there was no evidence to suggest that their rates were unduly influencing other RWAs. Indeed the fact that the highest paying RWA was in the vanguard of those wishing to abandon national negotiations indicates that the desire for local autonomy, together with the perceived opportunities offered by privatisation, were the crucial considerations rather than rates of pay.

The starting point for future negotiations in the industry is the 1989 agreement, although some divergence had already occurred by the date of its termination (Northumbrian for example introduced a 'Big Team Bonus' in 1988). It is likely that the decline in the number of manual and craft workers will lead to an early harmonisation of service conditions between these groups and, subsequently, between them and white collar workers. A further outcome of the general decline in the manual workforce is the greater significance of NALGO who claim to represent 45 per cent of the workers compared to 33 per cent in GMB, 15 per cent in NUPE and 5 to 6 per cent in TGWU. The ending of the national agreement substantially undermined the rationale for separate negotiating bodies for manual, craft and white collar employees. Senior staff had already been lifted out of national negotiations during the latter years of the 1980s and it is likely that the employers will eventually wish to negotiate with their workers as a single entity rather than along the stratified lines previously adopted. The proposed merger between NALGO and NUPE will remove one obstacle to harmonisation although this process might be at the expense of GMB. A further likely development is the extension of performance related pay, which is already in place for senior managers in some of the PLCs. It is also likely that profit sharing bonus schemes will be adopted.

On the union side the manual worker unions (i.e. GMB, NUPE and TGWU) have put forward a 'core' claim for 1990–91 and have maintained the notion of national bargaining through the National Trade Union Co-ordinating Committee for Industrial Staff in the Water Industry. On balance it appears unlikely that major changes in the trade unions recognised for negotiating purposes will occur (the NRA for example is prepared to recognise the unions which have traditionally dominated the industry), although some rationalisation may occur where very small numbers of craft employees are involved and currently organized by AEU, EETPU and UCATT. The position of MATSA may also be in question. Changes in working practices, greater flexibility and harmonisation may provide the unions with the opportunity of achieving their long term ambition to gain parity with workers in electricity supply and the gas industry. However, this may be at the cost of further job losses. It is probable that increasing technical sophistication in the industry will stimulate the need for further training and this may well involve negotiations with the recognised trade unions. Although, at the time of writing, the employers are currently keen to go it alone it would be foolish to rule out the possibility of the establishment of an employers' forum or even the return to some form of national negotiations.

Notes and references

1. Smith D. *The Rise and Fall of Monetarism*, Harmondsworth 1987.
2. Stewart M. *Keynes and After*, Harmondsworth 1987 edition.
3. Yarrow G. 'The Regulation of a Privatised Electricity Supply Industry' in Ramanadham V. *Privatisation in the UK*, 1988.
4. Ricard J. 'Privatisation in the Transport Sector' in Ramanadham op cit.
5. Jackson P. 'Economic Trends and Outlook' in *The Public Services Yearbook 1990*, 1990. The level of unemployment is a matter of controversy. For example, official figures claim a rate of 13.5 per cent at the height of unemployment in 1985 whereas the Unemployment Unit claim a rate of 15.3 per cent.
6. Taylor J. 'The Trade Union Problem Since 1960' in Pimlott B. and Cook C. (eds.) *Trade Unions in British Politics*, 1982.
7. Pagnamenta P. and Overy R. *All Our Working Lives*, 1984.
8. Palmer G. *British Industrial Relations*, 1983.
9. Hartley J., Kelly J. and Nicholson N. *Steel Strike: A Case Study in Industrial Relations*, 1983.
10. Op cit.
11. Adeney M. and Lloyd J. *The Miners' Strike 1984–5: Loss Without Limit*, 1987.
12. Op cit.
13. Riddell P. *The Thatcher Decade*, Oxford 1989.
14. For a full account see Sheldrake, J. 'The Water Industry: A Brief Review of its Development and Prospects' in London Review of Public Administration, August 1985.

Chapter 7

Conclusions

This book has traced the ebb and flow of governmental responsibility for industrial relations issues during the period 1880 to 1979. It has also noted the determination of the Thatcher Governments since the latter date to decisively divest themselves of such responsibility by seeking to restore the centrality of the market. Responsibility in this context relates to the perceptions of the electorate rather than more direct considerations such as intervention or ownership. We have noticed the early development of the legislative framework which provided the trade unions with the legal immunities that partially neutralised the underlying inequality between capital and labour. We have also observed that it was during the period immediately preceding the First World War that the Liberal Government introduced a series of measures aimed at mitigating the worst consequences of unemployment and poverty which are now recognised as the foundations of the welfare state. These measures (including the creation of labour exchanges, the development of unemployment insurance and the statutory imposition of minimum pay levels for certain groups of workers) signalled a growing acceptance that employment and, by extension, industrial relations issues were a legitimate concern of government and should not be left entirely to the vagaries of the market.

The forces urging government towards greater involvement in industrial relations were diverse and often contradictory.

Although in certain industries (e.g. engineering) industrial relations were highly developed there remained a residual hostility to trade unions among many employers (e.g. the railways). Indeed, as we have seen, such hostility together with a series of adverse judicial decisions culminating in the Taff Vale judgement, generated the desire on the part of many trade unions to obtain greater representation in Parliament as a means of extending legal immunities for their actions; a goal substantially achieved with the passage of the Trade Disputes Act 1906. However, while certain sections of the labour movement were embarking on a parliamentary road, other elements were encouraged to exploit the extra-parliamentary opportunities provided by industrial unrest to stimulate radical social change. Indeed, the use of the imported ideas of industrial unionism and syndicalism to provide an ideological underpinning for endemic labour unrest was perceived by government as a potent threat to political stability. The growing propensity of government to intervene in industrial relations was given tangible form in attempts by the Labour Department of the Board of Trade to enhance and extend the traditional form of negotiation which had developed during the nineteenth century. Briefly, the view emerged that the best industrial relations practices were those developed through the process of collective bargaining carried out by voluntary associations of employers and trade unions. The institutionalisation of conflict and the development of a constitutional approach to employment relationships were considered a bulwark against more dangerous alternatives. Nevertheless, prior to 1914 direct government intervention in industrial relations remained minimal and took the form of providing residual protection for selected workers through trade boards and offering conciliation in the more serious industrial disputes.

The First World War led to a rapid extension of governmental intervention in industrial relations. Labour shortages, the enhanced strength of the trade unions and the involvement of union leaders in government, provided the background for a concerted effort to transform the relationship between employers and employed on a lasting basis. This attempt was crystalised in the reports of the Whitley Committee published during 1917

and 1918. As we have seen, the Whitley Scheme was rejected by
the major industries and made its greatest impact in the public
utilities where it ultimately provided the basic configuration of
industrial relations. The proposals of the Whitley Committee
were, of course, built on optimistic assumptions concerning
the development of Britain's post-war economy. In the event,
a brief post-war boom was followed by rapid recession, a
disastrous general strike in 1926 and further trade depression
after 1929. The widespread unemployment of the inter-war years,
although it had its worst effects in Britain's staple industries,
substantially blighted attempts at radical reform of industrial
relations generally. Whilst efforts continued to encourage the
adoption of Whitleyism, attempts to bring the whole of industry
into an institutionalised network of negotiating practice failed.
Governments were initially unable and subsequently unwilling
to take the political risks involved in greater intervention.

The onset of the Second World War and the imposition of
a centrally controlled, command economy brought an end to
governmental hesitancy in matters of industrial relations policy.
Perhaps for the first time Britain experienced absolute manpower
shortage and adopted techniques of manpower planning quite
alien to her voluntaristic tradition. Government's necessarily
close engagement with labour enhanced the power of the
trade unions and laid the foundations of a post-war political
consensus built, above all, on a policy of full employment. As
we have noted successive governments in the post-war period
sought to maintain full employment through the application of
Keynesian economic techniques. Full employment enhanced the
bargaining power of organised labour and the strength of the
trade unions was increasingly cited as a factor in Britain's poor
economic performance vis-a-vis her competitors. Anxiety about
the economy became linked to the country's apparently poor
industrial relations record and efforts to improve the former
tended to include attempts to reform the latter. Significantly,
whereas government had already taken on the task of maintaining
full employment it now moved towards accepting electoral
responsibility for the efficient working of employment relationships based firmly on traditions of voluntarism and free
collective bargaining. Irrespective of political party, the response

of successive governments remained substantially the same. Firstly, efforts were made to reform industrial relations practice through legal intervention as a means of obtaining greater discipline, certainty and control. Secondly, attempts were made through the use of incomes policy to curb wage inflation. As we have seen, these policies were pursued by the governments of Wilson, Heath and Callaghan without success and ended with the defeat of the Labour Government in 1979.

Since 1979 the post-war consensus concerning full employment has been abandoned and government has attempted to expose the labour force to the constraints of the market. The extent to which the present government can claim that its policies have been successful remains open to debate. At the time of writing the general level of inflation and the level of pay increases are both disappointingly high at around 10 per cent. What is certain, however, is that government has made a decisive break with the approach to industrial relations which developed incrementally during the previous eighty years. The threat and reality of unemployment has radically reduced the bargaining strength of the trade unions and the prestige of the TUC. In a series of statutes the Conservative Governments of Margaret Thatcher have carried through a redefinition of the scope of trade union activity. Further, the problems of organised labour have been compounded by the heavy defeat of the Labour Party in the general elections of 1983 and 1987. The combined effects of historically high levels of unemployment, legislation hostile to labour and rapid technological change have injected far greater flexibility into the labour market with concomitant increases in the levels of productivity in many industries. The cost, however, in social and economic terms has been high. Indeed, continuing unemployment and the decline in Britain's manufacturing base are likely to figure among the key issues on which the next general election will be fought. In spite of a lingering nostalgia for the post-war consensus in some quarters, the extent to which it can now be realistically restored is problematical given the continuing vulnerability of the British economy and the many changes wrought since 1979. It is accurate to state that the Thatcher Government has now succeeded in distancing itself from the day to day flux of industrial relations issues. To this extent they are free from the close identification with the outcome of industrial disputes which served to undermine the authority of government during the Wilson, Heath and Callaghan years. Should the Conservatives remain in power after the next general election the policies pursued during the past ten years will no doubt be continued. Whether such policies (including further privatisation, efforts to obtain greater labour market flexibility and the underlying threat of unemployment) will prove sufficient to halt Britain's relative economic decline remains, however, open to question.

Select Bibliography

The place of publication is London unless stated otherwise.

Chapter 1

Fox A. *History and Heritage: The Social Origins of the British Industrial Relations System*, 1985.
Greenleaf, W. *The British Political Tradition* Volume 1 (The Rise of Collectivism) and Volume 2 (The Ideological Heritage), 1983.
Middlemas, K. *Politics in Industrial Society: The Experience of the British System Since 1911*, 1979.
Vickerstaff, S. and Sheldrake, J. *The Limits of Corporatism: The British Experience in the Twentieth Century*, Aldershot 1989.

Chapter 2

Armytage, W. H. G. *A. J Mundella 1825–1897*, 1951.
Askwith, Lord, *Industrial Problems and Disputes*, 1920.
Black, C. and Meyer, C. *Makers of Our Clothes: A Case for Trade Boards*, 1909.
Briggs, A. *Victorian People*, Harmondsworth 1965 edition.
Briggs, A. and Saville, J. (eds) *Essays in Labour History 1886–1923*, 1971.
Brown, K. (ed.) *Essays in Anti-Labour History*, Connecticut 1974.
Brown, K. (ed.) *The First Labour Party 1906–14*, 1985.
Burgess, K. *The Origins of British Industrial Relations: The Nineteenth*

Century Experience, 1975.

Dangerfield, G. *The Strange Death of Liberal England*, New York 1961 edition.

Davidson, R. *Whitehall and the Labour Problem in Late Victorian and Edwardian Britain*, 1985.

Drake, B. *Women in Trade Unions*, 1984 edition.

Ensor, R. C. K. *England 1870–1914*, Oxford 1936.

Ewing, K. *Trade Unions, the Labour Party and the Law*, Edinburgh 1982.

Harris, J. *Unemployment and Politics: A Study in English Social Policy 1886–1914*, Oxford 1972.

Harrison, R. *Before the Socialists*, 1965.

Haw, G. *The Life Story of Will Crooks*, 1917.

Hobsbawm, E. *Labouring Men*, 1964.

Holton, B. *British Syndicalism 1900–1914*, 1976.

Howell, G. *The Conflicts of Capital and Labour*, 1878.

Howell, G. *Labour Legislation, Labour Movements, Labour Leaders*, 1902.

Hunt, E. *British Labour History 1815–1914*, 1981.

Joyce, P. *Work, Society and Politics: The Culture of the Factory in Later Victorian England*, Brighton 1980.

Leventhal, F. *Respectable Radical: George Howell and Victorian Working Class Politics*, 1971.

Lichtheim, G. *A Short History of Socialism*, Glasgow 1975.

Lovell, J. *Stevedores and Dockers: A Study of Trade Unionism in the Port of London 1870–1914*, 1969.

MacKenzie, N. and MacKenzie, J. *The First Fabians*, 1979.

MacKenzie, N. and MacKenzie, J. (eds) *The Diary of Beatrice Webb* Volume 1 (1873–1892), 1982 and Volume 2 (1892–1905), 1983.

Morris, J. *Women Workers and the Sweated Trades*, Aldershot 1986.

Pelling, H. *The Origins of the Labour Party 1880–1900*, Oxford 1965 edition.

Pelling, H. *Popular Politics and Society in Late Victorian Britain*, 1968.

Perkin, H. *The Origins of Modern English Society 1780–1880*, 1972.

Phelps Brown, E. *The Growth of British Industrial Relations*, 1959.

Phelps Brown, H. *Origins of Trade Union Power*, Oxford, 1983.

Pugh, P. *Educate, Agitate, Organize: 100 Years of Fabian Socialism*, 1984.

Radice, E. and Radice, G. *Will Thorne: Constructive Militant*, 1974.

Radice, L. *Beatrice and Sidney Webb: Fabian Socialists*, 1984.

Roberts, B. *The Trades Union Congress 1868–1921*, 1958.

Schmiechen, J. *Sweated Industries and Sweated Labour: The London Clothing Trades 1860–1914*, Beckenham 1984.

Schneer, J. *Ben Tillett*, Beckenham 1982.

Shannon, R. *The Crisis of Imperialism 1865–1915*, 1976.

Sheldrake, J. *Municipal Socialism*, Aldershot 1989.
Stedman Jones, G. *Outcast London*, Oxford 1971.
Thompson, P. *Socialists, Liberals and Labour: The Struggle for London 1885–1914*.
Thorne. W. *My Life's Battles*, 1989 edition.
Vincent, A. and Plant, R. *Philosophy, Politics and Citizenship*, Oxford 1984.
Webb, B. *Our Partnership*, Cambridge 1975 edition.
Webb, S. *Socialism in England*, 1890.
Webb, S. and Webb B. *The History of Trade Unionism*, 1912 edition.
Wolfe, W. *From Radicalism to Socialism*, Yale 1975.
Wrigley, C. (ed.) *A History of British Industrial Relations*, Volume 1 1875–1914, Brighton 1982.

Chapter 3

Adams, R. *Arms and the Wizard*, 1978.
Amulree, Lord *Industrial Arbitration in Great Britain*, 1929.
Bayliss, F. *British Wages Councils*, Oxford 1962.
Burk, K. (ed.) *War and the State*, 1982.
Butler, H. *Confident Morning*, 1950.
Currie, R. *Industrial Politics*, Oxford 1979.
Goodrich, C. *The Frontier of Control*, New York 1921.
Harris, J. *William Beveridge: A Biography*, Oxford 1977.
Hinton, J. *The First Shop Stewards' Movement*, 1973.
Johnson, P. B. *Land Fit for Heroes: The Planning of British Reconstruction*, Chicago 1968.
Leventhal, F. *Arthur Henderson*, Manchester 1989.
Leggett, F. *Report on the Establishment and Progress of Joint Industrial Councils*, 1923.
Marwick, A. *The Deluge: British Society and the First World War*, 1965.
Morgan, K. *Consensus and Disunity: The Lloyd George Coalition Government 1918–1922*, Oxford 1979.
Morgan, K. and Morgan, J. *Portrait of a Progressive: The Political Career of Christopher Viscount Addison*, Oxford 1980.
Pribicevic, B. *The Shop Stewards' Movement and Workers' Control 1910–1922*, Oxford 1959.
Sells, D. *The British Trade Boards System*, 1923.
Seymour, J. *The Whitley Council Scheme*, 1932.
Sheldrake, J. and Vickerstaff, S. *The History of Industrial Training in Britain*, Aldershot 1987.
Sheldrake, J. *The Origins of Public Sector Industrial Relations*, Aldershot 1988.

Wright, A. *G. D. H. Cole and Social Democracy*, Oxford 1979.
Wrigley, C. *David Lloyd George and the British Labour Movement*, Brighton 1976.

Chapter 4

Addison, P. *The Road to 1945: British Politics and the Second World War*, 1975.
Aldcroft, D. *The Inter-War Economy: Britain 1919–39*, 1970.
Aldcroft, D. *From Versailles to Wall Street 1919–29*, Harmondsworth 1977.
Bellof, M. *Wars and Welfare: Britain 1914–45*, 1984.
Booth, A. and Pack, M. *Employment, Capital and Economic Planning: Great Britain 1918–39*, Oxford 1985.
Briggs, A. and Saville, J. (eds) *Essays in Labour History 1918–39*, 1977.
Bullock, A. *The Life and Times of Ernest Bevin* Volumes 1 and 2, 1960 and 1967.
Burgess, K. *The Challenge of Labour*, 1980.
Calder, A. *The People's War: Britain 1939–45*, 1969.
Charles, R. *The Development of Industrial Relations in Britain 1911–39*, 1973.
Citrine, Lord *Men and Work*, 1964.
Clay, H. *The Problem of Industrial Relations*, 1929.
Cowling, M. *The Impact of Labour 1920–24*, Cambridge 1971.
Davison, R. *British Unemployment Policy Since 1930*, 1938.
Hinton, J. *Labour and Socialism: A History of the British Labour Movement 1867–1974*, Brighton, 1983.
Ince, Sir G. *The Ministry of Labour and National Service*, 1960.
Inman, P. *Labour in the Munitions Industries*, 1957.
Lee, J. *The Churchill Coalition 1940–45*, 1980.
Lovell, J. *British Trade Unions 1875–1933*, 1977.
Mass Observation, *War Factory*, 1987 edition.
McKibbin, R. *The Evolution of the Labour Party 1910–24*, Oxford 1974.
Mowat, C. L. *Britain Between the Wars 1918–40*, 1968.
Parker, A. *Manpower: A Study of Wartime Policy and Administration*, 1957.
Pelling, H. *A Short History of the Labour Party*, 1982 edition.
Richardson, J. *Industrial Relations in Great Britain*, 1938.
Sells, D. *British Wages Boards: A Study in Industrial Democracy*, 1939.
Sharp, I. *Industrial Conciliation and Arbitration in Great Britain*, 1950.

Stevenson, J. *British Society 1914–1945*, Harmondsworth 1984.
Stevenson, J. and Cook C. *The Slump*, 1979.
Symons, J. *The General Strike*, 1987 edition.
Taylor, A. J. P. *English History 1914–45*, Oxford 1965.
Thorpe, A. *The Failure of Political Extremism in Inter-War Britain*, Exeter 1989.
Wigham, E. *Strikes and the Government 1893–1981*, 1982.
Wrigley, C. (ed.) *A History of British Industrial Relations*, Volume 2 1914–39, Brighton, 1987.

Chapter 5

ACAS *Industrial Relations Handbook*, 1980.
Bain, G. (ed.) *Industrial Relations in Britain*, Oxford 1983.
Bain, G. and Elsheikh, F. *Union Growth and the Business Cycle*, Oxford 1976.
Barnes, D. and Reid, E. *Governments and Trade Unions: The British Experience 1964–1979*, 1980.
Beer, S. *Modern British Politics*, 1969.
Blake, R. *The Conservative Party from Peel to Thatcher*, 1985.
Brown, W. (ed) *The Changing Contours of British Industrial Reltions*, Oxford 1981.
Calvocoressi, P. *The British Experience 1945–75*, 1978.
Crouch, C. *The Politics of Industrial Relations*, 1982.
Donoughue, B. *Prime Minister*, 1987.
Flanders, A. *The Fawley Productivity Agreements: A Case Study of Management and Collective Bargaining*, 1964.
Flanders, A. *Industrial Relations: What is Wrong with the System?*, 1965.
Guillebaud, C. *The Wages Councils System in Great Britain*, 1958.
Harris, K. *Attlee*, 1984 edition.
Holmes, M. *The Labour Government 1974–79*, 1985.
Jenkins, P. *The Battle of Downing Street*, 1970.
Leys, C. *Politics in Britain*, 1983.
Macdonald, D. *The State and the Trade Unions*, 1976 edition.
Martin, R. *New Technology and Industrial Relations in Fleet Street*, Oxford 1981.
Martin, R. M. *TUC: The Growth of a Pressure Group 1868–1976*, Oxford 1980.
Marwick, A. *British Society Since 1945*, Harmondsworth 1982.
Moran, M. *The Politics of Industrial Relations: The Origins, Life and Death of the 1971 Industrial Relations Act*, 1977.
Morgan, K. *Labour in Power 1945–51*, Oxford 1984.
Palmer, G. *British Industrial Relations*, 1983.

Pelling, H. *A History of British Trade Unionism*, Harmondsworth 1976 edition.
Pelling, H. *The Labour Governments 1945–51*, 1984.
Sked, A. and Cook, C. *Post-War Britain*, Harmondsworth 1984 edition.
Stewart, M. *Keynes and After*, Harmondsworth 1987 edition.
Weekes, B. et al *Industrial Relations and the Limits of Law: The Industrial Relations Effects of the Industrial Relations Act 1971*, Oxford 1975.
Whitehead, P. *The Writing on the Wall*, 1986 edition.

Chapter 6

Adeney, M. and Lloyd, J. *The Miners' Strike 1984–5: Loss Without Limit*, 1986.
Bassett, P. *Strike Free*, 1987.
Beer, S. *Britain Against Itself*, 1982.
Bell, D. *The Conservative Government 1979–84*, Beckenham 1985.
Coates, K. and Topham, T. *Trade Unions in Great Britain*, 1988.
Cole, J. *The Thatcher Years*, 1987.
Hartley, J. Kelly, J. and Nicholson, N. *Steel Strike: A Case Study in Industrial Relations*, 1983.
Holmes, M. *The First Thatcher Government 1979–1983*, Brighton 1985.
Jenkins, P. *Mrs Thatcher's Revolution*, 1989 edition.
Kavanagh, D. *Thatcherism and British Politics*, Oxford 1987.
Kavanagh, D. and Seldon, A. (eds) *The Thatcher Effect: A Decade of Change*, Oxford 1989.
Leys, C. *Politics in Britain*, 1983.
MacGregor, I. *The Enemies Within, The Story of the Miners Strike 1984–5*, 1986.
MacInnes, J. *Thatcherism at Work*, Milton Keynes 1987.
Marquand, D. *The Unprincipled Society* 1988.
Pagnamenta, P. and Overy, R. *All Our Working Lives*, 1984.
Ramanadham, V, *Privatisation in the UK*, 1988.
Riddell, P. *The Thatcher Government*, Oxford 1985.
Riddell, P. *The Thatcher Decade*, Oxford 1989.
Saran, R. and Sheldrake, J. (eds) *Public Sector Bargaining in the 1980s*, Aldershot 1988.
Skidelsky, R. (ed.) *Thatcherism*, 1988.
Smith, D. *The Rise and Fall of Monetarism*, Harmondsworth 1987.
Taylor, A. *Trade Unions and Politics*, 1989.

Index